SpringerBriefs in Environment, Security, Development and Peace

Volume 34

Series Editor

Hans Günter Brauch, Peace Research & European Security Studies, Mosbach, Baden-Württemberg, Germany

More information about this series at http://www.springer.com/series/10357
http://www.afes-press-books.de/html/SpringerBriefs_ESDP.htm
http://www.afes-press-books.de/html/SpringerBriefs_ESDP_34.htm

Myint Zan
Editor

Legal Education and Legal Traditions: Selected Essays

Springer

Editor
Myint Zan
Faculty of Law
Multimedia University
Malacca, Malaysia

More on this book is at: http://www.afes-press-books.de/html/SpringerBriefs_ESDP_34.htm

ISSN 2193-3162 ISSN 2193-3170 (electronic)
SpringerBriefs in Environment, Security, Development and Peace
ISBN 978-3-030-50902-6 ISBN 978-3-030-50903-3 (eBook)
https://doi.org/10.1007/978-3-030-50903-3

Copy editing: PD Dr. Hans Günter Brauch, AFES-PRESS e.V., Mosbach, Germany
English Language Editor: Mr. Stewart Manley, Lecturer, Faculty of Law, University of Malaya, Kuala Lumpur, Malaysia

This Springer imprint is published by the registered company Springer Nature Switzerland AG
The registered company address is: Gewerbestrasse 11, 6330 Cham, Switzerland

Acknowledgements

The preparation for and production of this book have been a long, arduous process which involved, among others, the editor communicating with about 16 persons from different countries for many months during this process.

The editor would like to express his sincere thanks to the ESDP Series Editor PD Dr. Hans Gunter Brauch and Mr. Stewart Manley, Lecturer, Faculty of Law, University of Malaya, for their kind assistance, cooperation and patience in the production of this book.

The editor is grateful to Dr. Johanna Schwarz and Dr. Christian Witschel of the Springer Nature Office in Heidelberg (Germany) and to the producers of this book, Ms. Birke Dalia (Germany) and Mr. Arulmurugan Venkatasalam (Chennai, India), and his team of typesetters in Chennai, Tamil Nadu (India).

Yangon, Myanmar
March 2020

Prof. Dr. Myint Zan (Retd.)

Contents

Part I
Legal Education

Chapter 1
Reflections on the Teaching of 1982 the Law of Sea Convention

Mary George

Abstract The importance of the Law of the Sea as a subject cannot be undermined. In particular, civil servants should audit this course where offered by their local universities as it informs them of a wide-ranging array of issues within the course that could help in their continuous professional development (CPD). The Faculty of Law at the University of Malaya is one example of a tertiary educational institution that offers the Law of the Sea.

Keywords Continuing Professional Development Course (at the University of Malaya) · 1982 Third United Nations Conference of the Law of the Sea (UNCLOS III) · 1992 United Nations Conference on Environment and Development · Maritime Zones · Navigation and Protection of the Marine Environment

1.1 Introduction

It is important for Malaysian civil servants to audit the Law of the Sea course, as offered at the University of Malaya, Faculty of Law, on payment of a fee, as compulsory curriculum in their continuous professional development (CPD). Though CPD is not part of the civil service culture yet, it is hoped that it will be at some point in the future. However, CPD is a well-established feature for the Malaysian lawyers. As provided by the Bar Council:

> The CPD Department was formed on October 2012 to ensure effective implementation of the CPD Scheme. It is dedicated to assist and support lawyers by providing a wide range of CPD activities in different practice areas through various training platforms. The CPD Department also focuses to ensure lawyers have regular access to essential information of the CPD Scheme.
>
> The main objectives of CPD Department are to:
>
> - offer legal training in a variety of practice areas with access to both local and international trainers;
> - develop educational structures that will allow lawyers to enhance their competence, skills and professional practice;

Professor Dr. Mary George, Faculty of Law, University of Malaya, Kuala Lumpur, Malaysia. Email: maryg@um.edu.my.

M. Zan (ed.), *Legal Education and Legal Traditions: Selected Essays*,
SpringerBriefs in Environment, Security, Development and Peace,
https://doi.org/10.1007/978-3-030-50903-3_1

- implement a structural framework that will minimise the need for lawyers to manage their own CPD tracking;
- create a platform for interaction between lawyers and the CPD Department in order to foster a lawyer-centric CPD environment; and
- provide opportunities that support lifelong learning.[1]

The Law of the Sea has been taught as a specialized LLM course at the Faculty of Law, University of Malaya. To enrol for this course, there is no pre-requisite to be fulfilled. This means that candidates enrolling for this subject, need not have passed an undergraduate course in Public International Law. The reason why there is no pre-requisite for the Law of the Sea course is because many of the students who register for a LLM programme are mature students, many being practitioners at the Bar who have not studied Public International Law. Students enrolled in the course are taken through the main provisions of public international law. Relevant case laws and other international instruments are also taught as necessary. Sometimes, students are exposed to other international law fields such as international arbitration or international environmental law, to help understand some of the public international law aspects of the Law of the Sea course.

For a sound understanding of this subject, a background knowledge of public international law, international relations, air law, space law, maritime terrorism laws and marine environmental law is desirabe. Some students are familiar with the *1972 Stockholm Declarationon the Environment*,[2] the *1992 United Nations Conference on Environment and Development*[3] held in Rio de Janeiro, Brazil in 1992 which adopted the concept of "sustainable development" embodied in Agenda 21. Chapter 17 of Agenda 21 focuses on the programme of action for the seas and oceans. Where this knowledge has been imparted to students, the March towards understanding a rational, prudent and balanced use of the ocean's resources is made easier. It is unrealistic to expect all students in Malaysia to have covered these areas in their undergraduate studies. The United Nations has through UNGA Resolution 25 September 2015 adopted the UN Agenda 2030, *Global Plan for Sustainable Development*. Therefore, the teaching of the Law of the Sea course at the postgraduate level adopts a two-pronged strategy. First, an explanation of the general rules of international law for example, why States comply with international law, the meaning of State sovereignty, and jurisdiction in the Law of the Sea. Secondly, it focuses on the technical aspects of the subject.

The syllabus for the Law of the Sea comprises:

---

[1]For the CPD Programme, see https://cpd.malaysianbar.org.my/ and https://cpd.malaysianbar.org.my/about-us/. The idea of a CPD Programme for the Malaysian Civil Service came from a discussion with MsAnneliz Reina George, Special Projects Executive Officer for the Bar Council of Malaysia, speaking in her personal capacity only and it does not represent the views of the organization she works at.

[2]*Declaration of the United Nations Conference on the Human Environment*, UN Doc A/RES/2994, 11 ILM 1416 (15 December 1972).

[3]UN Doc. A/CONF.151/26, 31 ILM 874 (13 June 1992).

1. the Hague Conference for the Codification of International Law[4] held in 1930 under the auspices of the League of Nations. This Conference dealt with the territorial waters. Although not agreeing on the breadth of the territorial sea, it could present in its report 13 draft articles setting out a measure of agreement on many aspects of this subject;
2. the four 1958 Geneva Conventions and the Optional Protocol[5] that were adopted on 29 April 1958, as recorded in the Final Act (A/CONF.13/L.58, 1958, UNCLOS, Off. Rec. vol. 2, 146), the United Nations Conference on the Law of the Sea (UNCLOS I):

    - the Convention on the Territorial Sea and the Contiguous Zone[6];
    - the Convention on the High Seas[7];
    - the Convention on Fishing and Conservation of the Living Resources of the High Seas[8];
    - the Convention on the Continental Shelf[9]; and
    - the Optional Protocol of Signature concerning the Compulsory Settlement of Disputes[10];

3. the 1982 Law of the Sea Convention (*1982 LOSC*, which was adopted at UNCLOS III).[11]
4. selected conventions of the International Maritime Organization for the safety of navigation and control of marine pollution[12] and the Food and Agricultural Organization for fisheries regulations.[13]

---

[4]League of Nations, Acts of the Conference for the Codification of International Law, v 1 (19 August 1930) https://biblio-archive.unog.ch/Dateien/CouncilMSD/C-351-M-145-1930-V_EN.pdf.

[5]Tullio Treves, '1958 Geneva Conventions on the Law of the Sea', United Nations Audiovisual Library of International Law http://legal.un.org/avl/pdf/ha/gclos/gclos_e.pdf 24 June 2018. The Convention on the Territorial Sea entered into force on 10 September 1964; the Convention on the High Seas on 30 September 1962; the Convention on Fishing and Conservation of the Living Resources of the High Seas on 20 March 1966; the Convention on the Continental Shelf on 10 June 1964; and the Optional Protocol of Signature concerning the Compulsory Settlement of Disputes on 30 September 1962.

[6]UNTS vol 516 (29 April 1958) 205.

[7]UNTS vol 450 (30 September 1962) 11.

[8]UNTS vol 559 (20 March 1966) 285.

[9]UNTS vol 499 (10 June 1964) 311.

[10]UNTS vol 450 (30 September 1962) 169

[11]UNTS 1833 (16 November 1994) 3, UNTS 1834 (16 November 1994) 3, UNTS 1835 (16 November 1994) 3; Agreement Relating to the Implementation of Part XI of the United Nations Convention on the Law of the Sea, UNTS 1836 (10 December 1982) 3.

[12]*Convention on the Prevention of Marine Pollution by Dumping of Wastes and Other Matter*, UNTS vol 1046 (29 December 1972) 120; International Convention for the Prevention of Pollution from Ships, UNTS vol 1340 (12 November 1973) 6, as modified by the Protocol of 1978 relating thereto, MARPOL 73/78 (17 February 1978).

[13]Agreement for the Implementation of the Provisions of the United Nations Convention on the Law of the Sea of 10 December 1982 relating to the Conservation and Management of Straddling Fish Stocks and Highly Migratory Fish Stocks, UNTS vol 2167 (4 August 1995) 3.

5. Any current Law of the Sea topic, for example, marine spatial planning or conflicts in the South China Sea or regulation of living resources in areas beyond national jurisdiction or any other topic that deserves to be brought to the attention of the postgraduate students.

Of all the conventions listed above, this chapter only focuses on the *1982 LOSC* which came into force on 16 November 1994, one year after Guyana became the 60th State to adhere to it. As of 23 September 2016, 168 States have ratified the Convention and implemented it bringing large tracts of the ocean under national sovereignty and jurisdiction. Archipelagic States have been recognized for the first time under the Convention. Under Article 311, paragraph 1, of the *1982 LOSC*, the *1982 LOSC* "shall prevail, as between States Parties, over the Geneva Conventions on the Law of the Sea of 29 April 1958". The 168 parties to the *1982 LOSC* include most of the States bound by the Geneva Conventions; the latter Conventions remain binding only as between, or in the relationships with, the few States that are parties to the relevant Geneva Convention and not parties to the *1982 LOSC*. This is, in particular, the case of the United States, Colombia, Israel and Venezuela.[14]

Much of the *1982 LOSC* represents a progressive development of the law with few customary international law provisions.

1.2 The 1982 LOSC: A Constitution for the Oceans

The *1982 Law of the Sea Convention*, has been heralded as a 'Constitution' for the oceans by the drafters of the Third United Nations Conference on the Law of the Sea.[15] The significance and import of this statement is best understood when we examine the lack of order on the seas before the *1982 LOSC*.[16] There are conflicts at sea even after the entry into force of the LOSC but many of these are deliberate breaches of the rule of law, whether of LOSC rules or rules of public international law. The salient features of the 1982 LOSC are the division of seas into maritime zones

---

[14]Treves (n 5).

[15]"A Constitution for the Oceans", Remarks by Tommy T.B. Koh, of Singapore, President of the Third United Nations Conference on the Law of the Sea: Adapted from statements by the President on 6 and 11 December 1982 at the final session of the Conference at Montego Bay. See United Nations Convention on the Law of the Sea at p. xxxiii.

[16]Tullio Treves, 'Historical Development of the Law of the Sea' in Donald Rothwell, Alex Oude Elferink, Karen Scott, and Tim Stephens (eds), *The Oxford Handbook of the Law of the Sea* (Oxford University Press, 2015) https://doi.org/10.1093/law/9780198715481.003.0001.

from internal waters to the exclusive economic zone and continental shelf[17]; navigation; protection of the marine environment[18]; deep-seabed mining and the exploitation regime[19]; marine scientific research[20] and settlement of disputes.[21] This paper focuses on the first three of these aspects. The deep-seabed mining provisions had engendered significant differences between developing and developed industrialized States which the Secretary-General resolved through a series of informal consultations among States resulting in the *1994 Agreement Related to the Implementation of Part XI of the LOSC*.[22]

1.3 A Snapshot of the Early Conflicts at Sea: Claims, Counterclaims and Sovereignty Disputes Over Resources and Territories

In 1494, the famous Papal Bull of Pope Alexander VI carved up the Atlantic Ocean between Spain and Portugal, the two dominant maritime powers of the period.[23] From the seventeenth to the early twentieth centuries, there was a great deal of freedom in the use of the seas. States were allowed to claim a narrow belt of the seas adjacent to their coasts as their territorial sea for purposes of exercising national jurisdiction over smugglers, warships and other intruders. This was followed by the "cannon-shot" rule that was popular in Europe in the eighteenth century which enabled States to fire cannons up to three nautical miles from shore for coastal defence, a feature very important to major maritime and naval powers.

---

[17]See Parts V and VI, *1982 LOSC*.

[18]See Part XII, *1982 LOSC*.

[19]Part XI, *1982 LOSC* and 1994 Implementing Agreement.

[20]Part XIII, *1982 LOSC*.

[21]Part XV, *1982 LOSC*.

[22]See n11.The then UN Secretary-General Javier Perez de Cuellar convened in July 1990 a series of informal consultations which culminated in the adoption, on 28 July 1994, of the Agreement relating to the implementation of Part XI of the United Nations Convention on the Law of the Sea of 10 December 1982.. The Agreement was adopted on 28 July 1994 and entered into force on 28 July 1996. It consists of 10 articles dealing mainly with procedural aspects such as signature, entry into force and provisional application. Its article 2 deals with the relationship between the Agreement and Part XI of the Convention and it provides that the two shall be interpreted and applied together as a single instrument. In the event of an inconsistency between the Agreement and Part XI, however, the provisions of the Agreement shall prevail. The Agreement has an annex, divided into nine sections, dealing with the various issues that were identified as problem areas during the informal consultations. These include costs to States Parties and institutional arrangements; decision-making mechanisms for the Authority; and future amendments of the Convention. See United Nations, Division of Ocean Affairs and the Law of the Sea, 'Oceans & the Law of the Sea' (online at 26 June 2018) http://www.un.org/depts/los/convention_agreements/convention_overview_part_xi.htm.

[23]*Treaty of Tordesillas*, Spain-Portugal (entered into force 1494) https://www.britannica.com/event/Treaty-of-Tordesillas.

When, in the twentieth century, States began to claim a 12-mile territorial sea, it was not welcomed by these Powers who feared that their freedom of navigation on the seas would be compromised. Where many coastal States desired extended maritime jurisdiction due to the impetus to claim principally fisheries resources, the major maritime and naval Powers wanted these curtailed. There were many challenges to closing the seas and leaving them open, resulting in the Closed Sea and Open Sea doctrines. Uncontrolled marine pollution stemming from operational and accidental spills from ships was on the rise. The oceans were a scene of conflict and instability by the mid-twentieth century.[24]

There were escalating tensions between coastal States and others relating to, amongst others, problems relating to sovereignty claims over islands and maritime features in the oceans, conflicting demands for fisheries oil, gas, tin, diamonds, gravel, metals/ minerals, and harvesting rich sea-bed resources on the sea floor. States responded unilaterally to these tensions, as for example, in 1945, President Harry S Truman, unilaterally extended United States jurisdiction over all natural resources on that nation's continental shelf – oil, gas, minerals, etc. which other nations soon followed.[25] Reports of the "Cod War" between Iceland and the United Kingdom and the *1969 North Sea Continental Shelf* cases decided by the International Court of Justice are proof of the chaos that was at sea (regarding disputes pertaining to the implementation of the Law of the Sea).[26]

The three Latin American States of Peru, Chile and Ecuador in the 1940s and 1950s claimed a 200 nautical miles (nms) zone to protect their fisheries which was incorporated in the *Santiago Declaration* of 1952.[27] This *Declaration* was endorsed by other Latin American States in the 1970 *Montevideo* Declaration[28] and *1970 Lima Declaration.*[29] What was needed on the seas was order, the rule of law and good faith among States.

The Third United Nations Conference on the Law of the Sea, UNCLOS III, was the first global diplomatic exercise on the basis of universal participatory democracy, to regulate the seabed and write rules for all ocean areas, all uses of the seas and all of its resources. UNCLOS III was convened in New York in 1973 just after the October 1973 Arab-Israeli war, with the oil embargo and high oil prices that sharpened interests over control of the continental shelf with its vast oil reserves.

[24]See generally, Hugo Grotius, *Mare Liberum(The Freedom of the Seas)*, Lodewijk Elzevir 1609; R.R. Churchill and A.V. Lowe, *The Law of the Sea* (Juris Publishing, Manchester University Press, 3rd ed, 1999).

[25]UC Santa Barbara, The American Presidency Project https://cil.nus.edu.sg/databasecil/1945-us-presidential-proclamation-no-2667-policy-of-the-united-states-with-respect-to-the-natural-resources-of-the-subsoil-and-sea-bed-of-the-continental-shelf/.

[26][1969] ICJ Rep 4.

[27]Declaration on the Maritime Zone, 1006(I) UNTS No 14758 (18 August 1952). https://treaties.un.org/doc/Publication/UNTS/volume%201006/volume-1006-I-14758-English.pdf.

[28]Montevideo Declaration on the Law of the Sea, 9 ILM 1081 (8 May 1970) https://iea.uoregon.edu/treaty-text/1970-montevideodeclarationlawofseaentxt.

[29]Declaration of the Latin American States on the Law of the Sea (10 August 1970) https://iea.uoregon.edu/treaty-text/1970-limadeclarationlawseaentxt.

Already, significant amounts of oil were coming from offshore facilities. Nine years later, the 1982 LOSC was adopted.[30]

1.4 Three Salient Features of the *1982 LOSC*

The three salient features of the *1982 LOSC* are:

1. Division of seas into maritime zones from internal waters to the exclusive economic zone and continental shelf.
2. Navigation.
3. Protection of the Marine Environment.

1.4.1 Division of Maritime Zones

The *1982 LOSC* separated the national and international waters as different States espoused different limits on the breadth of their territorial seas ranging from 3 to 200 nms with naval and maritime powers seeking limits on these territorial sea claims. The *1982 LOSC* established a uniform 12-mile territorial sea where States enjoy sovereignty and other 12-mile contiguous zone jurisdiction where States enjoy customs, sanitary, immigration and fiscal jurisdiction for any violation of the laws of the coastal State within its territory or the territorial sea.

The issue of straits that were used for international navigation was problematic at UNCLOS III between major naval powers and coastal States as the former equated the straits as high seas and the latter feared for their national security. While there is an overlap of the territorial sea and a strait used for international navigation, some might argue otherwise upon an examination of Part III on *Straits Used for International Navigation*. A 12-mile territorial sea would place under national jurisdiction of coastal States:

- the Strait of Gibraltar (8 miles wide and the only open access to the Mediterranean),
- the Strait of Malacca (20 miles wide and the main sea route between the Pacific and Indian Oceans),
- the Strait of Hormuz (21 miles wide and the only passage to the oil-producing areas of Gulf States)
- Bab el Mandeb (14 miles wide, connecting the Indian Ocean with the Red Sea).

For purposes of the special navigational regime of the straits, the territorial sea and the straits are different, whereas for all other purposes, they may be considered the same even though the language of the *1982 LOSC* does not necessarily support this inference.

[30] *1982 LOSC* (n 11) and related UNCLOS III Proceedings.

The next maritime zone is a unique zone of 200 nautical miles called, the exclusive economic zone (EEZ), where States enjoy specific sovereign and economic rights and jurisdiction. Previously this area represented the High Seas. This gives 38 million square nautical miles of ocean space per State. Consequently, almost all known and estimated maritime hydrocarbon reserves fall under national jurisdiction.

In the EEZ, *1982 LOSC* recognizes sovereign rights for exploitation of fisheries, oil and gas, water, currents and winds; construction of artificial islands and platforms, conduct of marine scientific research and jurisdiction with regard to establishment and use of artificial islands, installations and structures, marine scientific research and the protection and preservation of the marine environment.

The disorderly nature and undefined procedures of the *1958 Convention on Fishing and Conservation of the Living Resources of the High Seas* stand in stark contrast. Under the *1958 Convention*, coastal States could take "unilateral measures" of conservation on the high seas, as considered then. Where a fisheries–sharing agreement between a coastal and a fishing nation was not negotiated within six months, the coastal State could impose terms of fishing. Rights and obligations under the *1958 Convention* were confusing and hardly enforced. Fishing disputes over cod, anchovies or tuna were so common then. In comparison, the *1982 LOSC* requires coastal States to give access to the surplus fisheries to the land-locked countries.

Equally important was the delimitation of the sea-bed of the continental shelf with its rich oil and gas reserves, minerals, immense quantities of sand, gravel, gold and diamonds. Notable oil and gas players have been the Middle East, Nigeria, Malaysia and Indonesia.

Countries with long coastlines and archipelagic States tend to benefit from the EEZ and continental shelf regimes. Where geologically blessed and subject to certain conditions, States could claim continental shelves up to 350 nautical miles.

The term 'continental shelf' got a new meaning in the *1982 LOSC* compared to earlier usage of the term in Article 1 of the *1958 Convention on the Continental Shelf*. "the seabed and subsoil of the submarine areas adjacent to the coast but outside the area of the territorial sea, to a depth of 200 metres, or, beyond that limit, to where the depth of the superjacent waters admits of the exploitation of the natural resources of the said areas".

The *1982 LOSC* defines the continental shelf of a coastal States as that comprising the seabed and its subsoil that extend beyond the limits of its territorial sea throughout the natural prolongation of its land territory to the outer edge of the continental margin, or to a distance of 200 nautical miles from the baselines from which the territorial sea is measured, where the outer edge of the continental margin does not extend up to that distance.

In cases where the continental margin extends further than 200 nautical miles, nations may claim jurisdiction up to 350 nautical miles from the baseline or 100 nautical miles from the 2500 metre depth, depending on certain criteria such as the thickness of sedimentary deposits.

The *1982 LOSC* therefore provides that the 200 nautical miles EEZ boundary applies to the continental shelf also. Some nations such as Argentina stood to gain from a broader continental shelf. An institution called the Commission on the Limits of the Continental Shelf has been set up under LOSC to consider continental shelf claims up to 350 nautical miles.

1.4.2 Navigation and Protection of the Marine Environment

All ships and submarines enjoy the right of "innocent passage" through the territorial seas so long as the coastal State's sovereignty is not threatened. States also have a right of transit passage through straits used for international navigation, such as the Straits of Malacca and Singapore. Likewise, archipelagic States have a 12 mile territorial sea, from a line drawn joining the outermost points of the outermost islands of the group that are in close proximity to each other. In straits used for international navigation, the new passage regime is called transit passage which required concessions from the major naval powers and the coastal States.

In the transit passage regime, the duties of coastal States resemble those of the territorial sea provisions while the freedom of navigation accorded to the user States resemble those of the high seas unimpeded freedoms of navigation and overflight. It was a difficult and unfair compromise for the coastal States as the obligations required from the user States were couched in non-mandatory language.

Moreover some of the navigation and prevention of marine pollution obligations that flag States have to observe stemmed from their being members and parties to the conventions of the International Maritime Organization that they had ratified.

The sea suffers from anthropogenic pollution stemming largely from land-based sources and also to some extent from ships. Examples of ship-based pollutants include, oil, chemicals, garbage, sewage, atmospheric emissions and dumping.

For the first time in history, *the 1982 LOSC* made it mandatory to prevent, reduce and control marine pollution of the seas and thereby to protect and preserve the marine environment. Coastal States are given the necessary prescriptive and enforcement jurisdiction for purposes of ship-based marine pollution control for enforcement under the Convention and for enforcement of "generally accepted international rules and standards" adopted by the International Maritime Organization.

An example in point is the "flag State" jurisdiction which empowers the flag State whose flag the ship flies to enforce the relevant laws on board the ship. Another device is called "port State" jurisdiction when the ship calls at a port. Port States are able to enforce treaty obligations that are implemented in national regulations dealing with shipping standards, marine safety and pollution prevention.

To avoid the use of force for a failure in negotiations or settlement of an issue, the *1982 LOSC* obliges States in advance to commit to settle their disputes and agreed to be bound by the decisions made in accordance with the dispute settlement provisions. It stresses the importance of binding settlements by third party judges, or arbitrators or by direct negotiation. It has set up a special tribunal for this purpose called the International Tribunal for the Law of the Sea (ITLOS) which offers another venue to litigious States Parties and a Seabed Disputes Chamber within it.

Under the *1982 LOSC*, States Parties may go to the ITLOS or the International Court of Justice (ICJ), or to general or special arbitration or to a Conciliation Commission that is to be followed by Negotiation of an Agreement under the Conciliation Commission Report.

The *1982 LOSC* has brought in its wake new maritime zones, concepts of jurisdiction and new uses of the ocean. This Convention has to be read with other multilateral obligations of States that they have contracted under other treaties that are compatible with the spirit and objective of LOSC. Finally, all of these provisions need to make their way into national legislation for effective implementation, followed by monitoring, enforcement and compliance.

In conclusion, given the currency of the issues discussed in the course, and given the fact that Malaysia is surrounded by the Straits of Malacca and Singapore, the Straits of Johore and the South China Sea, and plays a leading role in many international fora, it is important for Malaysian civil servants to audit this course as part of their continuous professional development.

Bibliography

Books

Birnie, Patricia and Alan Boyle, *International Law and the Environment* (Oxford University Press, 2nd ed, 2001)
Brownlie, Ian, *Principles of Public International Law* (Oxford University Press, 7th ed, 2008)
Churchill, R.R. and A.V. Lowe, *The Law of the Sea* (Manchester University Press, 3rd ed, 1999)
Davenport, Tara, Ian Townsend-Gault, Clive Schofield and Leonardo Bernard (eds), *Beyond Territorial Disputes in the South China Sea* (Edward Elgar, 2013).
Dixon, Martin, *Textbook on International Law* (Oxford University Press, 6th ed, 2007)
George, Mary, *The Legal Regime Straits of Malacca* (Lexis Nexis, 2008)
Grotius, Hugo, *Mare Liberum* (The Freedom of the Seas), 1609
Harris, D.J., *Cases and Materials on International Law* (Sweet and Maxwell, 7th ed, 2010)
Keyuan, Zou, *China's Marine Legal System and the Law of the Sea* (MartinusNijhoff, 2005)
Nien-Tsu, Alfred Hu and Ted L. McDorman (eds), *Maritime Issues in the South China Sea: Troubled Waters or a Sea of Opportunity* (Routledge, 2013)
Sohn, Louis B., John E. Noyes, Erik Franckx, Kristen Gustafson (eds), *Cases and Materials on the Law of the Sea* (Brill Nijhoff, 2nd ed, 2014)
Song, Yann-huei and Keyuan Zou, *Major Law and Policy Issues in the South China Sea: European and American Perspectives*(Ashgate Publishing, 2014)
Treves, Tullio, 'Dispute-Settlement in the Law of the Sea: Disorder or System?' in M. G. Kohen (ed), *Promoting Justice, Human Rights and Conflict Resolution through International Law / La promotion de la justice, des droits de l'homme et du règlement des conflits par le droit international* (Brill Nijhoff, 2007)

International Conventions and Agreements

Charter of the United Nations, San Francisco, 26 June 1945
Convention between the United States of America and Mexico Relating to the Establishment of an International Commission for the Scientific Investigation of Tuna, Mexico City, 25 January 1949, 99 UNTS 3
The 1982 Law of the Sea Convention and related UNCLOS III Proceedings
Convention between the United States of America and the Republic of Costa Rica for the Establishment of an Inter-American Tropical Tuna Commission, Washington DC, 31 May 1949, 80 UNTS
Convention on the High Seas, Geneva, 29 April 1958, 450 UNTS
Convention on the Continental Shelf, Geneva, 29 April 1958, 499 UNTS
Convention on the Territorial Sea and the Contiguous Zone, Geneva, 29 April 1958, 516 UNTS 205
Convention on Fishing and Conservation of the Living Resources of the High Seas, Geneva, 29 April 1958, 559 UNTS 285
Optional Protocol of Signature concerning the Compulsory Settlement of Disputes, Geneva, 29 April 1958, 450 UNTS 169
Vienna Convention on Diplomatic Relations, Vienna, 18 April 1961, 500 UNTS 95
International Convention for the Conservation of Atlantic Tunas, Rio de Janeiro, 14 May 1966, 673 UNTS 63
Vienna Convention on the Law of Treaties, Vienna, 23 May 1969, 1155 UNTS 331
Convention on the Prevention of Marine Pollution by Dumping of Wastes and other Matter, London, Mexico City, Moscow, Washington D.C., 29 December 1972, 1046 UNTS 120
International Convention for the Prevention of Pollution from Ships, London, 2 November 1973, 1340 UNTS 184
Protocol of 1978 relating to the International Convention for the Prevention of Pollution from Ships, London, 17 February 1978, 1340 UNTS 61
International Convention for the Safety of Life at Sea, London, 1 November 1974, 1184 UNTS 277
United Nations Convention on the Law of the Sea, Montego Bay, 10 December 1982, 1833 UNTS 3
Convention for the Conservation of Southern Bluefin Tuna, Canberra, 10 May 1993, 1819 UNTS 359
Agreement Relating to the Implementation of Part XI of the United Nations Convention on the Law of the Sea of 10 December 1982, New York, 28 July 1994, 1836 UNTS 3
Agreement for the Implementation of the Provisions of the United Nations Convention on the Law of the Sea of 10 December 1982 relating to the Conservation and Management of Straddling Fish Stocks and Highly Migratory Fish Stocks, New York, 4 August 1995, 2167 UNTS 3

Articles

Treves, Tullio, 'Conflicts between the International Tribunal for the Law of the Sea and the International Court of Justice' (1999) 31 *NYU Journal of International Law & Politics* 809
Treves, Tullio, 'Flags of Convenience before the Law of the Sea Tribunal' (2004) 6 *San Diego International Law Journal* 179

Other

Oceans & Law of the Sea Convention, Division for Ocean Affairs and Law of the Sea: *Chronological Lists of, Accessions and Successions to the Convention and Related Documents*, https://www.un.org/depts/los/reference_files/chronological_lists_of_ratifications.htm

Chapter 2
The Future of Lawyers as Transaction Cost Engineers

Dennis Wye Keen Khong

Abstract This paper explains the important role lawyers play as 'transaction cost engineers', in facilitating negotiations and in contracting. It analyses the significant contributions made by Ronald H. Coase on the importance of paying attention to transaction costs, as well as the lessons that can be derived from the so-called Coase Theorem. It also looks at the role contemporary lawyers can and should play outside of a litigation setting, as well as the nature of legal education on training lawyers as transaction cost engineers. The opportunities brought about by the increased use of information technology in legal practice are also considered.

Keywords Ronald Coase · Coase Theorem · 'The Nature of the Firm' · Lawyers as transaction cost engineers · Legal education · Law tech

2.1 Ronald H. Coase

In 1931, a young London School of Economics undergraduate student named Ronald Coase won a travelling scholarship to the United States to study the structure of industries, which in essence, was on the question of why firms exist.[1] It was very fashionable back then to hold the view that the pricing system of the free market, following on Adam Smith's metaphor of the 'invisible hand',[2] is the only necessary coordinating mechanism in the production process. However, one question kept puzzling Coase: if a price system can do all the coordination, why do firms still exist? Why is it still necessary to have command and control within businesses? Shouldn't every individual be just an independent contractor?

Dr. Dennis Wye Keen Khong, Associate Professor, Faculty of Law, Multimedia University, Malacca, Malaysia, Email: wkkhong@mmu.edu.my.

[1] R. H. Coase, 'The Institutional Structure of Production' (1992) 82(4) *American Economic Review* 713.

[2] Adam Smith, *An Inquiry into the Nature and Causes of the Wealth of Nations* (W Strahan and T Cadell, 1776) bk 4 ch 2: 'As every individual, therefore, endeavours as much as he can both to employ his capital in the support of domestic industry, and so to direct that industry that its produce may be of the greatest value; every individual necessarily labours to render the annual revenue of

M. Zan (ed.), *Legal Education and Legal Traditions: Selected Essays*,
SpringerBriefs in Environment, Security, Development and Peace,
https://doi.org/10.1007/978-3-030-50903-3_2

So, armed with some letters of recommendation, Coase visited many great American manufacturers and interviewed notable industrialists of the day to discuss the many functions of a firm, and to look for the answer to his question. After a year of investigation, Coase came back with a surprisingly simple answer: transaction cost. He found that using the market is not free. Although businessmen knew intuitively that contracting is a costly process, economics textbooks have traditionally assumed away the existence of transaction cost. In other words, the existence of firms is given, but not questioned.

Coase has never in his writings given a detailed definition for the phrase 'transaction cost'. The closest he has done so was to describe transaction cost as the 'cost of using the price mechanism'.[3] From this definition, we understand 'transaction cost' as to mean the costs of transferring property rights.[4] Examples of these costs are the searching cost for contracting parties, negotiation cost of contracts, legal cost in drafting agreements, and monitoring and enforcement costs of contract performance.

Firms exist because it is cheaper to enter into long-term relational contracts for labour. Businesses enjoy savings by vertically integrating different processes, e.g. from design to manufacturing, from marketing to distribution, to ensure certainty of supply and flexibility in responding to the changing trends and tastes of the consumer market.[5] Upon urging of his colleagues, Coase wrote up his idea and published it in a paper titled 'The Nature of the Firm' in the 1937 volume of *Economica*.[6]

Fast forward to 1959. By now, Coase has married an American woman and migrated to the United States, and was then at the University of Virginia. In the same year, he published a paper on the Federal Communications Commission in the then newly established *Journal of Law and Economics*, on the issue of conflicting uses of radio spectrum.[7] Coase referred to a student article on allocation of colour television radio spectrum published in the *University of Chicago Law Review* eight years earlier than his own article published in 1959,[8] and recommended that the

---

the society as great as he can. He generally, indeed, neither intends to promote the public interest, nor knows how much he is promoting it. By preferring the support of domestic to that of foreign industry, he intends only his own security; and by directing that industry in such a manner as its produce may be of the greatest value, he intends only his own gain, and he is in this, as in many other cases, led by an invisible hand to promote an end which was no part of his intention. Nor is it always the worse for the society that it was no part of it. By pursuing his own interest he frequently promotes that of the society more effectually than when he really intends to promote it'.

[3] R. H. Coase, 'The Nature of the Firm' (1937) 4(16) *Economica* 386, 390.

[4] Jürg Niehans, 'Transaction Costs', *The New Palgrave: A Dictionary of Economics* (Macmillan Press 1987) 676; Douglas W. Allen, 'Transaction Costs', *Encyclopedia of Law and Economics* (Edward Elgar Publishing 2000) 893.

[5] Benjamin Klein, Robert G. Crawford and Armen A. Alchian, 'Vertical Integration, Appropriable Rents, and the Competitive Contracting Process' (1978) 21(2) *Journal of Law and Economics* 297; see also, Ronald Coase, 'The Conduct of Economics: The Example of Fisher Body and General Motors' (2006) 15(2) *Journal of Economics & Management Strategy* 255.

[6] Coase, 'The Nature of the Firm' (n 3) 386.

[7] R. H. Coase, 'The Federal Communications Commission' (1959) 2 *Journal of Law and Economics* 1.

[8] Leo Herzel, '"Public Interest" and the Market in Color Television Regulation' (1951) 18(4) *University of Chicago Law Review* 802.

efficient solution to radio spectrum is to auction the radio frequencies to the highest bidder.

Coase introduced an innovation in the way he wrote his Federal Communications Commission paper. He referred to the English nuisance case of *Sturges v Bridgman*,[9] where the court held that a defendant confectioner was liable for nuisance when his machinery was interfering with the plaintiff's use and enjoyment of the adjoining property, even though the defendant had been in business decades earlier than the plaintiff. Coase then co-opted the facts of that case to illustrate the point that if parties could bargain, an economically superior outcome could be achieved. Unfortunately, bargaining as a preferred solution ran contrary to the perceived economic wisdom of the time. It is thought that the State, a regulator or a judge should intervene by preventing the nuisance maker from interfering with the enjoyment of rights of his neighbours.

After the publication of the Federal Communications Commission paper, a group of renowned economists at the University of Chicago started to have some doubts as to the correctness of Coase's proposition. Coase was invited to take a trip to Chicago to discuss his ideas. It was stated that at the beginning of the evening, a straw poll was taken and all the participants were found to be against Coase's idea. Then, after some lengthy deliberation, they were won over one by one by Coase, and by the end of the evening, a second straw poll showed a unanimous agreement with Coase. Coase was then urged to write up his ideas in another paper to be published in the following issue of the *Journal of Law and Economics*.[10]

'The Problem of Social Cost' remains Ronald H. Coase's most famous work.[11] Although not strictly a legal doctrinal piece, according to data compiled and analysed by two law librarians at the Yale Law School and the Harvard Law School, Coase's 'The Problem of Social Cost' is the most cited law review paper of all time.[12]

'The Problem of Social Cost' also brought renewed attention to the then forgotten 'The Nature of the Firm' paper. More importantly, 'The Problem of Social Cost' was the catalyst which started the law and economics movement, first, in the United States and then in Europe. It demonstrated that by careful study of case law, an economist may create new knowledge for both legal scholars and economists alike.

Today, Coase's two seminal papers are considered as the forefathers of various fields of research, such as law and economics, new institutional economics, and transaction cost economics. Not many scholars can claim to have played as pivotal a role as Coase in enriching and enhancing the insights into legal scholarship from the related discipline of economics. In 1991, Coase won the Sveriges Riksbank Prize

---

[9](1879) 11 Ch D 852.

[10]George J. Stigler, *Memoirs of an Unregulated Economist* (University of Chicago Press, 2003) 76: 'We strongly objected to this heresy. Milton Friedman did most of the talking, as usual. He also did much of the thinking, as usual. In the course of two hours of argument the vote went from twenty against and one for Coase to twenty-one for Coase. What an exhilarating event! I lamented afterward that we had not had the clairvoyance to tape it.'

[11]Ronald H. Coase, 'The Problem of Social Cost' (1960) 3 *Journal of Law and Economics* 1.

[12]Fred R. Shapiro and Michelle Pearse, 'The Most-Cited Law Review Articles of All Time' (2012) 110(8) *Michigan Law Review* 1483.

in Economic Sciences in Memory of Alfred Nobel, or commonly known as the Nobel Prize for economics, for 'his discovery and clarification of the significance of transaction costs and property rights for the institutional structure and functioning of the economy'.

2.2 The Coase Theorem

The essence of Ronald Coase's message in the 'The Problem of Social Cost' paper is that transaction cost matters in ensuring whether, in a conflict of resource use situation, negotiation will lead to an efficient use of resources. According to Coase, the primary role of law, regulators and the legal system should be to reduce transaction cost.

George Stigler, another Nobel Prize winner and a famous economist, took Coase's proposition one step further and created the Coase Theorem, by hypothesizing on what happens when transaction cost is zero.[13] According to the Stigler's 'Coase Theorem', when transaction cost is zero, and property rights is clearly defined, the final allocation of property rights is efficient, and is the same, irrespective of the initial allocation of property rights.

To use an example, suppose that there are two neighbours: one loves to play the piano while another loves solitude. If nuisance law says that it is the right of the solitude-lover to enjoy his quietness, then the piano player will have to negotiate with his neighbour or to find an alternative solution. Options open to the piano-lover include paying off the neighbours so that he does not file a complaint, building a soundproof wall, moving away, paying the neighbours to move away, buying a digital piano with a headphone, or stop playing the piano altogether. Obviously the final solution depends on how much the piano player values his playing, how much the solitude-lover values his solitude and how much the various solutions will cost the piano player. If say, the piano player values his playing high enough, and the cheapest solution in the list is to buy a digital piano, the piano-player will choose the cheapest and the most efficient solution, i.e. buying a digital piano. Zero transaction cost means that there is no barrier to bargaining, all price information is available without any costs, and the solitude-lover does not mislead the piano player on how much he values, in monetary terms, his solitude.

The interesting point, as postulated by the Coase Theorem, is that the same efficient solution will be arrived at even if the law says that the piano player has a right to play his piano and the solitude-lover could not stop the piano buyer without paying him off. In this case, when the solitude-lover looks at the same list of options, he too

[13]George J. Stigler, *The Theory of Price* (Macmillan Publishing, 3rd ed, 1966) 113: 'The Coase theorem thus asserts that under perfect competition private and social costs will be equal'; George J. Stigler, *The Theory of Price* (Macmillan Publishing, 4th ed, 1987) 322: '[T]he "Coase Theorem" … asserts that legal rules would have no influence upon the use of resources in a world of zero transaction costs'.

will want to buy a digital piano for the piano-playing-lover, for that is the cheapest solution for him.

Therefore, the Coase Theorem states that if parties could bargain and weigh the various options, an efficient final solution will be achieved. The initial allocation of property rights is not important in terms of achieving an efficient solution, as long as some allocation of property rights is made. Conversely, if the law is ambiguous about the initial allocation of property rights, then parties will have no choice but to litigate, solely to determine the initial allocation.

Initial allocation of property rights matters in relation to the question of who pays, i.e. the distribution question, although in a world of zero transaction cost, it has no effect on efficiency. Using the analogy of a pie, efficiency is about making the size of the pie as big as possible, and distribution is about who gets a bigger slice of the pie.

The Coase Theorem tells us that the law and the legal system should strive to do two things: allocate property rights and lower transaction costs.

It has to be noted at this point that in the real world, we do not always find zero or even low transaction cost situations. The case of *Lord Bernstein of Leigh v Skyviews & General Ltd.*[14] illustrates this point. In *Lord Bernstein* the issue before the court was whether a landowner enjoys a right against trespass to his airspace without any limitations, or whether that right is only to a reasonable height, and that an aeroplane flying overhead does not infringe the landowner's right to the enjoyment of his airspace.

Consider the transaction cost involved in establishing an airway if landowners have a right to airspace without any limitation or only to a reasonable height. The value of airways and flight paths to airlines and society is obviously very high. On the other hand, the reasonable utility of airspace at such high altitude is minuscule or practically zero. However, if individual landowners may strategically block the formation of such airways by demanding a price, the collective value demanded to pay off the landowners will exceed the value of the airways to the airlines and passengers, which then results in the inability of contracting an airway for the airlines.[15] Therefore, in such situations, Coase's preposition fails, and we will have to rely on alternative solutions. One is attributed to the seventeenth century English philosopher Thomas Hobbes: "Structure the law so as to minimize the harm caused by failures in private agreements." In other words, Hobbes' precept asks us not to focus on reducing transaction cost, but focus on allocating property rights to the party who values it the most, i.e. the airlines, when private bargaining is impossible.[16] Fortunately, the court in *Lord Bernstein* reached the same solution even without recourse to an explicit transaction cost argument.

---

[14] [1978] QB 479.

[15] Ben Depoorter and Sven Vanneste, 'Putting Humpty Dumpty Back Together: Experimental Evidence of Anticommons Tragedies' (2006) 3(1) *Journal of Law, Economics & Policy* 1.

[16] Robert Cooter, 'The Cost of Coase' (1982) 11(1) *The Journal of Legal Studies* 1; Robert Cooter and Thomas Ulen, *Law & Economics* (Pearson, 6th ed, 2012) 92.

Hobbes' solution is not the only way out of a conundrum such as in *Lord Bernstein*. An alternative method is to avoid bargaining altogether and require the party taking away the property rights to pay for those rights. Taking a cue from road accident cases, Calabresi and Melamed revealed another transaction cost insight through what they call liability rules protection of property rights.[17] According to them, not all situations permit bargaining which arrives at an efficient use of property rights. In some situations, such as accidents, it is impossible to have a pre-accident contract with everyone. In others, property rights owners may demand a ransom price instead of a normal market price from a potential efficient user, such as a provider of public infrastructure. Therefore, liability rules for protection of property rights allows the state to transfer the property rights to a public use by paying compensation at a rate determined by a neutral third party or by operation of some statutory laws.[18] In Malaysia, such powers can be found in the *Land Acquisition Act 1960* (*Act 486*).

2.3 Lawyers as Transaction Cost Engineers

Apart from the lofty goals of upholding justice, defending innocent clients, challenging administrative wrongdoings and protecting human rights, lawyers, particularly solicitors, in the English sense of the term, play a very important role as what Ronald J. Gilson called 'transaction cost engineers'.[19]

Lawyers build no bridges or skyscrapers. They don't create works of art which inspire generations to come. They don't manufacture useful widgets which will make our lives easier. But some lawyers are arguably 'creators' nevertheless. Some lawyers do 'create', effect or produce deals.

Using their knowledge and skills in negotiating and creating contracts, lawyers enable the movement and use of resources in a potential mutually beneficial way to the contracting parties. The common forms of contracts which create deals include property conveyancing, tenancies and leases, sales and purchase of goods, construction, franchising, insurance, financing, intellectual property licensing, trusts, etc. Although 'boilerplate agreements' are easily available, lawyers still have a role to play in ensuring that proper due diligence is conducted and specific terms are crafted in a legally enforceable and to the fullest extent possible unambiguously.

Lawyers as transaction cost engineers have to ensure that risks are properly defined and allocated, the duty to disclose information held by a party which is material to the contract is specified, and the time frame for performance and delivery is achievable. It goes without saying that the lawyer as a transaction cost engineer has to have a good

[17]Guido Calabresi and A. Douglas Melamed, 'Property Rules, Liability Rules, and Inalienability: One View of the Cathedral' (1972) 85(6) *Harvard Law Review* 1089.

[18]Thomas J. Miceli and Kathleen Segerson, 'The Economics of Eminent Domain: Private Property, Public Use, and Just Compensation' (2007) 3(4) *Foundations and Trends® in Microeconomics* 275.

[19]Ronald J. Gilson, 'Lawyers as Transaction Cost Engineers' in Peter Newman (ed), *The New Palgrave Dictionary of Economics and the Law* (Palgrave Macmillan, 1998).

working knowledge of the relevant law, and if the agreement is trans-jurisdictional, also has the pre-requisite knowledge of all relevant domestic and international laws.

No contract is perfectly contingent, i.e. able to covers all possible and improbable eventualities. Therefore, the transaction cost lawyers have to ensure that their clients are not exposed to crippling high risks and liabilities. In other words, commercial lawyers as transaction cost engineers, must know how to assess and manage contractual risks. In short, they play a very important role in society as the facilitators of deals which allows new creations beneficial to members of the society.

Lawyers, as transaction cost engineers, may also play a role in reducing the transaction cost in another way, namely by creating an efficient and low transaction cost legal system. Going back to Coase's precept, the role of legal system in ensuring an efficient outcome is two-fold: allocate property rights, and reduce transaction costs. Therefore, there is a role for lawyers, as transaction cost engineers, to facilitate the design of a legal system which reduces transaction cost.

Legislation can play an important role in reducing transaction costs in the market. Compulsory information-disclosure rules require businesses, and sometimes consumers, to disclose information that they have in order to overcome problems associated with information asymmetry and to facilitate consumers making optimal choices in their purchases.[20] Examples of such information-forcing rules can be found in the *Consumer Protection Act 1999* (Act 599), *Insurance Act 1996 (Act 553) National Land Code, and Trade Description Act 2011* (*Act 730*).

Another example of a genre of law reducing transaction cost is contract law. In its most fundamental form, contract law plays the role of enforcing agreements, without which, it would be difficult or even risky to enter into agreement to transfer or exchange property rights. As we have seen, exchanges increase social welfare. So contract law enables exchanges by securing enforceable agreements between parties to a contract.

2.4 Training of the Transaction Cost Engineers

When we start to recognise that the lawyers do not only have multiple social roles but also have an equally important economic role in society, we will then have to ask the inevitable question of how to train lawyers to be effective transaction cost engineers.[21] The following suggestions can be made.

No doubt, understanding of some basic economic theories will be helpful. The lawyer as a transaction cost engineer has to understand prevailing business practices and accounting rules. Knowledge of finance is also useful in dealing with risks and

[20] Michael J. Trebilcock, 'Rethinking Consumer Protection Policy' in Charles E. F. Rickett and Thomas G. W. Telfer (eds), *International Perspectives on Consumers' Access to Justice* (Cambridge University Press, 2003) 68.

[21] Lisa Bernstein, 'The Silicon Valley Lawyer as Transaction Cost Engineer?' (1995) 74 *Oregon Law Review* 239.

financial instruments. In general, lawyers should be trained, in addition to the usual legal domain, knowledge of business administration. It is therefore not surprising, that to enhance the value of their graduates, some American law schools offer joint degrees in JD and MBA.

In the context of Malaysian legal education, law students aspiring to be transaction cost engineers should be trained in business negotiation skills, risk assessment and management, and commercial legal practices. This last part will require students to be active learners by drafting contracts of various kinds. It is therefore insufficient for students to undergo just a course in contract law. A commercial drafting course will have to concentrate on contract drafting. Students have to dissect in detail standard 'boilerplate' contracts. A business case method of teaching may also be explored where students are given real business situations and are required to draft risk-reducing, efficient contracts.

Textbooks on contract law may have to be re-written to focus on the above mentioned skills: negotiation, risk management, contract drafting. There should be a conscious move away from doctrinalism and steer towards a modern form of American legal realism.[22] Real life business cases can be used in these textbooks. The choice of contract terms has to be explained and the various risks and potential costs, involved in different types of terms, made clear.

Disputes and disagreements are if not inevitable, most likely to occur. One of the roles of the transaction cost engineer is to settle disputes and disagreements, such that the parties reach a consensus and a contract can be drawn. Mediation and negotiation skills become important skills of a transaction cost engineer.

Training of lawyers as transaction cost engineers is not something we are used to doing in a typical Bachelor of Laws programme. The underlying design of a law degree still very much mirrors the training of an advocate. We should recognise that lawyers can and should also be deal-makers seeking, in certain contexts mainly though not exclusively in commercial laws and their implementation and practice for 'win-win situations'. Prevention is better than cure. Law is not just litigation. In the real world, non-litigation legal work outnumbers litigation work.

2.5 Lawtech Comes to the Transaction Cost Engineer

Industry 4.0 refers to the industrial change where big data, automation, artificial intelligence and smart devices play an important role in the day-to-day life of the people.[23] It is expected that this change will permeate through the whole of human civilisation, and no industry will escape its overwhelming impact. Many traditional jobs will disappear after being replaced by machines and automation. As of now,

[22] See Wilfrid E. Rumble, 'Legal Realism', *Encyclopedia of the American Constitution* (Macmillan Reference USA, 1986) http://www.encyclopedia.com/politics/encyclopedias-almanacs-transcripts-and-maps/legal-realism.

[23] Klaus Schwab, *The Fourth Industrial Revolution* (World Economic Forum, 2016).

repetitive work and work requiring classification are routinely being automated by artificial intelligence technology. The legal profession is not immune to this onslaught of technological advancement. It is myopic to argue that the legal profession is different and continue to operate as it has in the past.

There is now an emerging field of industry called lawtech or legal technology.[24] Software developers are joining hands with legal specialists to develop software solutions for the legal industry. This goes beyond the traditional word processor, accounting software and case management system. Recent advancements include contract analysis, legal chatbots, document management and search tools, and e-discovery tools.[25]

Richard Susskind predicts eight new jobs in the legal profession, one of them is the 'legal knowledge engineer'.[26] According to him, the role of the legal knowledge engineer is to analyse, distil, and capture legal knowledge into computer systems. Also, the legal practitioners of the future is expected to lower the cost of legal advice and processes by employing online systems to provide commodified legal services, as opposed to bespoke services on a one-to-one basis.[27]

Law schools now have a role to prepare future law graduates to navigate this uncharted terrain. The exact need and nature of future legal practice remain uncertain. However, it is wrong to just to turn a blind eye to this impending challenge and maintain the *status quo* in legal education, by not taking proactive steps to prepare law students as future legal practitioners. Given that machine learning and deep learning technologies are being used in various applications of artificial intelligence, it might be necessary to expose law students to the practical sides and ethical issues of artificial intelligence.

One possibility is to have specialised technical modules which train law students to become legal knowledge engineers. Students should be exposed to different forms of knowledge systems, such as expert systems, document assembly systems, chatbots and technology-assisted review systems. Apart from knowing how these systems work, it is perhaps necessary to train law students to be sufficiently competent in translating legal knowledge into a technical solution using one of these techniques. It is advisable to have an even more ambitious programme which teaches components of programming and artificial intelligence. Students in engineering schools

---

[24] Some people believe that there is a difference between the terms 'lawtech' and 'legal-tech', such that the former covers disruptive technologies which bypass the use of lawyers, whereas the latter is confined to technologies used by lawyers. See The Law Botique, 'Is There a Difference Between LawTech and LegalTech?', *medium.com* (6 December 2018) https://medium.com/@thelawboutiquelondon/is-there-a-difference-between-lawtech-and-legaltech-68f776d5ab98.

[25] See The Law Society, 'Lawtech Adoption Research' (14 February 2019) https://www.lawsociety.org.uk/support-services/research-trends/lawtech-adoption-report/.

[26] Richard Susskind, *Tomorrow's Lawyers: An Introduction to Your Future* (Oxford University Press, 2013); Richard E Susskind, 'Expert Systems in Law: A Jurisprudential Approach to Artificial Intelligence and Legal Reasoning' (1986) 49(2) *Modern Law Review* 168.

[27] Richard Susskind, *The Future of Law: Facing the Challenges of Information Technology* (Clarendon Press, 1996).

are taught sufficient amount of programming knowledge such that they are technically competent to develop hardware solutions with embedded computer programs. It is advisable that at least some law students who intended to be 'transaction cost engineers' be acquainted with such knowledge.

The transition from a transaction cost engineer qua engineer to a legal knowledge engineer of the future is a natural progression. It is expected that increase use of automation will reduce the cost of providing legal services leading to the reduction of the transaction costs of using the legal system. Automating legal processes should be seen in a positive light, because it would mean that more property rights are transferred and the welfare of the society is enhanced.

2.6 Conclusion

Ronald H. Coase has started the movement some eighty years ago with his idea of transaction cost. With globalisation already prevalent in many parts of the planet, vast amount of information at our finger-tips, and potential deals at all four corners of the world, twenty four hours a day, seven days a week, the time is now to acknowledge lawyers especially in certain aspects of law can and should be transaction cost engineers. Law faculties have to take up this challenge and prepare law students for this role.

Ronald H. Coase is no longer with us. He passed away on 2 September 2013 at the ripe old age of 102. His legacy in law and in economics will be well-remembered for a very long time. Training law students to become and facilitating lawyers' role as transaction cost engineers would be a tribute to the memory of Ronald Coase and his interdisciplinary contributions to legal knowledge.

Bibliography

Books

Allen, Douglas W, 'Transaction Costs', *Encyclopedia of Law and Economics* (Edward Elgar Publishing 2000)

Cooter, Robert and Thomas Ulen, *Law & Economics* (Pearson, 6th ed, 2012)

Encyclopedia of Law and Economics (2000)

Gilson, Ronald J, 'Lawyers as Transaction Cost Engineers' in Peter Newman (ed), *The New Palgrave Dictionary of Economics and the Law* (Palgrave Macmillan, 1998)

Newman, Peter (ed), *The New Palgrave Dictionary of Economics and the Law* (Palgrave Macmillan, 1998)

Niehans, Jürg, 'Transaction Costs', *The New Palgrave: A Dictionary of Economics* (Macmillan Press 1987)

Rickett Charles E F and Thomas GW Telfer (eds), *International Perspectives on Consumers' Access to Justice* (Cambridge University Press, 2003)

Rumble, Wilfrid E, 'Legal Realism', *Encyclopedia of the American Constitution* (Macmillan Reference USA, 1986) http://www.encyclopedia.com/politics/encyclopedias-almanacs-transcripts-and-maps/legal-realism
Schwab, Klaus, *The Fourth Industrial Revolution* (World Economic Forum, 2016)
Smith, Adam, *An Inquiry into the Nature and Causes of the Wealth of Nations* (W Strahan and T Cadell, 1776)
Stigler, George J, *Memoirs of an Unregulated Economist* (University of Chicago Press, 2003)
Stigler, George J, *The Theory of Price* (Macmillan Publishing, 3rd ed, 1966)
Stigler, George J, *The Theory of Price* (Macmillan Publishing, 4th edition, 1987)
Susskind, Richard, *The Future of Law:* Facing the Challenges of Information Technology (Clarendon Press, 1996)
Susskind, Richard, *Tomorrow's Lawyers: An Introduction to Your Future* (Oxford University Press, 2013)
Trebilcock, Michael J, 'Rethinking Consumer Protection Policy' in Charles E F Rickett and Thomas G W Telfer (eds), *International Perspectives on Consumers' Access to Justice* (Cambridge University Press, 2003)

Cases

Lord Bernstein of Leigh v Skyviews & General Ltd [1978] QB 479
Sturges v Bridgman (1879) *11 Ch D 852*

Articles

Bernstein, Lisa, 'The Silicon Valley Lawyer as Transaction Cost Engineer?' (1995) 74 *Oregon Law Review* 239
Calabresi, Guido and A Douglas Melamed, 'Property Rules, Liability Rules, and Inalienability: One View of the Cathedral' (1972) 85(6) *Harvard Law Review* 1089
Coase, R H, 'The Federal Communications Commission' (1959) 2 *Journal of Law and Economics* 1
Coase, R H, 'The Institutional Structure of Production' (1992) 82(4) *American Economic Review* 713
Coase, R H, 'The Nature of the Firm' (1937) 4(16) *Economica* 386
Coase, Ronald H, 'The Problem of Social Cost' (1960) 3 *Journal of Law and Economics* 1
Coase, Ronald, 'The Conduct of Economics: The Example of Fisher Body and General Motors' (2006) 15(2) *Journal of Economics & Management Strategy* 255
Cooter, Robert and Thomas Ulen, *Law & Economics* (Pearson, 6th ed, 2012) 92
Cooter, Robert, 'The Cost of Coase' (1982) 11(1) *The Journal of Legal Studies* 1
Depoorter, Ben and Sven Vanneste, 'Putting Humpty Dumpty Back Together: Experimental Evidence of Anticommons Tragedies' (2006) 3(1) *Journal of Law, Economics & Policy* 1
Herzel, Leo, '"Public Interest" and the Market in Color Television Regulation' (1951) 18(4) *University of Chicago Law Review* 802
Klein, Benjamin, Robert G Crawford and Armen A Alchian, 'Vertical Integration, Appropriable Rents, and the Competitive Contracting Process' (1978) 21(2) *Journal of Law and Economics* 297
Miceli, Thomas J and Kathleen Segerson, 'The Economics of Eminent Domain: Private Property, Public Use, and Just Compensation' (2007) 3(4) *Foundations and Trends® in Microeconomics* 275

Shapiro, Fred R and Michelle Pearse, 'The Most-Cited Law Review Articles of All Time' (2012) 110(8) *Michigan Law Review* 1483

Susskind, Richard E, 'Expert Systems in Law: A Jurisprudential Approach to Artificial Intelligence and Legal Reasoning' (1986) 49(2) *Modern Law Review* 168

Other

The Law Botique, 'Is There a Difference Between LawTech and LegalTech?', *medium.com* (6 December 2018) https://medium.com/@thelawboutiquelondon/is-there-a-difference-between-lawtech-and-legaltech-68f776d5ab98

The Law Society, 'Lawtech Adoption Research' (14 February 2019) https://www.lawsociety.org.uk/support-services/research-trends/lawtech-adoption-report/

Chapter 3
Human Values in Legal Professionals' Ethics Education

Gita Radhakrishna

Abstract Education has been variously defined in dictionaries as the act or process of educating or being educated in a certain aspect of knowledge or skill through a specific programme of instruction on the one hand and on the other as an instructive or enlightening experience. The Sai Spiritual Education defines 'education' as 'opening wide the doors of the mind, cleansing the inner tool of consciousness, the senses, ego and reason'. Sri Sathya Sai Baba, the founder of the Education in Human Values program says that education is for cultivating both the mind and the heart. It is to raise children with a lively conscience so that they can discern Truth from untruth, Eternal from transient, right from wrong, and so guide their lives grounded in peace, love, joy and harmony. The program is founded on the five core human values of truth, right conduct, love, peace and non-violence. The UNESCO Report on Education for the Twenty-first Century, states that 'humankind sees in education an indispensable asset in its attempt to attain the ideals of peace, freedom and social justice'. The Commission is of the view that while education is a continuous process of improving knowledge and skills, it is also a means of bringing about personal development and fostering peace, understanding and harmony among individuals and nations. Legal Professional ethics is a compulsory course for qualifying law undergraduates. This paper examines the correlation between these core human values and legal professional ethics to determine whether this would lead to better ethics in the legal profession and awareness of their ethical responsibilities to society. These cover a spectrum of duties from the duty of a counsel to the court, to the client, to opposing counsel, the special duties of criminal lawyers and duty of counsel to society in general. The very fact that legal professional ethics has to be included in the syllabus for a law degree indicates the recognition of a dire erosion in professional values in society today. Learning and understanding professional ethics makes a positive contribution to enabling students understand their role as lawyers and become constructive citizens.

Keywords Human values · Education · Legal professional ethics · Malaysian legislation concerning legal ethics · Case law concerning legal ethics and lawyer's duties · Continuing professional development

Dr. Gita Radhakrishna, Senior Lecturer, Faculty of Law, Multimedia University, 75450 Malacca, Malaysia Email gita.radhakrishna@mmu.edu.my.

M. Zan (ed.), *Legal Education and Legal Traditions: Selected Essays*,
SpringerBriefs in Environment, Security, Development and Peace,
https://doi.org/10.1007/978-3-030-50903-3_3

3.1 Introduction

The legal profession has, at times, been the butt of jokes. The public perception of lawyers has generally been negative, as people who obfuscate matters and distort the truth to suit their ends. In the light of these views generally held by the public a canvassing of views, opinions and regulations to discern what should be the legal professional ethics is necessary. Lord Denning when delivering a lecture on Legal Professional Ethics stated:

> If there is one thing more important than any other in a lawyer, it is that he should be honest. He must be honest with his client. He must be honest with his opponent. He must be honest with the court. Above all, he must be honest with himself.[1]

The quotation very aptly sets out the basic responsibilities of a lawyer i.e. to the court, to his client, to fellow brethren and to society. Professional Practice,[2] is a compulsory paper for final year law undergraduates in most Malaysian universities. This paper examines the correlation between education in human values and legal professional ethics and whether its study has enabled law students to understand their ethical professional responsibilities. A qualitative research methodology has been adopted. The basis of Sri Sathya Sai Baba Education in Human Values is studied and compared to the ethics underlying the legal profession in Malaysia, as set out in the *Malaysian Legal Profession Act 1976, Legal Profession (Practice & Etiquette) Rules 1978* (LEPPER) and the *Legal Profession (Publicity) Rules 2001* (LEPUB).

3.2 Education in Human Values

Education has been variously defined in dictionaries as the act or process of educating or being educated in a certain aspect of knowledge or skill through a specific program of instruction on the one hand and on the other as an instructive or enlightening experience.[3] The Sai Spiritual Education defines 'education' as 'opening wide the doors of the mind, cleansing the inner tool of consciousness, the senses, ego and reason'.[4] Values are the 'principles and fundamental convictions which act as general guides to behavior, the standards by which particular actions are judged as good or

---

[1]Lord Denning, 'The Honest Lawyer' (1983) 2 *Current Law Journal* 174.

[2]The subject may have different names in different universities.

[3]*The American Heritage Dictionary of the English Language* (Houghton Mifflin Company, 4th ed, 2009) http://www.thefreedictionary.com/education; Lexico.com http://www.oxforddictionaries.com/definition/english/education.

[4]Sri Sathya Sai Baba, *Sri Sathya Sai University* (2007) 103 http://www.sathyasai.org/files2007/globaloverview/chapter5_30jun07.pdf.

desirable'.[5] Life without proper values would be chaotic and disastrous.[6] Sri Sathya Sai Baba, the founder of the Education in Human Values says that education is for cultivating both the mind and the heart. It is to raise children with a lively conscience so that they can discern truth from untruth, eternal from transient, right from wrong, and so guide their lives grounded in peace, love, joy and harmony.[7] The program is founded on the five core human values of truth, right conduct, love, peace and non-violence. Coincidentally, the UNESCO Report on *Education for the Twenty-first Century*, states that 'humankind sees in education an indispensable asset in its attempt to attain the ideals of peace, freedom and social justice'.[8] The Commission views education as serving the twin purpose of continuously improving knowledge and skills. At the same time education should also foster personal development as well as peace, understanding and harmony among individuals and nations.

The SSE program develops discrimination and greater alertness, helping one to make reasoned, inner choices rather than acting automatically from habit or custom without any understanding. The focus is on five basic universal human values.[9] Truth is the first and foremost value in shaping character. In the words of Sir Walter Scott

> O, what a tangled web we weave;
> When first we practice to deceive![10]

Lying hurts ourselves as well as others. Victims of lies suffer upon finding out because they feel deceived and manipulated. They may then doubt their own ability to assess the truth and make reasoned decisions. They could become untrusting and they could also seek revenge. The liar is also hurt because he has to remember the lies he had said, act in conformity to these, continue to lie to avoid detection and be wary of those he had lied to. His credibility and integrity is damaged and he may become a habitual liar and go on to commit other wrongs.[11]

The next core value is 'right conduct' which covers both our physical and mental spheres: a healthy body leads to a healthy mind. On the physical level, students are exposed to basic hygiene, healthy diet and the importance of daily exercise. On the mental level, good thoughts (imbibed through the five senses) and good company

---

[5]J Mark Halstead and Monica J. Taylor, 'Learning and Teaching about Values: A Review of Recent Research' (2000) 30(2) *Cambridge Journal of Education* 169.

[6]J Lakshmi, 'Innovative and Best Practices in Teaching of Value Education' (2014) 2(5) *Tactful Management Research Journal* 1 http://oldtm.lbp.world/UploadedArticles/125.pdf.

[7]https://www.acnc.gov.au/charity/c60a8ff5fcc64949bb303ce4b73ba462.

[8]Jacques Delors, 'Learning: The Treasure Within; Report to UNESCO of the International Commission on Education for the Twenty-first Century (highlights)' (UNESCO Publishing, 1996) https://unesdoc.unesco.org/ark:/48223/pf0000109590.

[9]The British Institute of Sathya Sai education in Human Values F:\Conferences\Educare Conference 2014\Articles\British Institute of Sathya Sai Education.htm [accessed 15 April 2014].

[10]Sir Walter Scott, *Marmion* (1808) Canto VI, Stanza 17 http://en.wikipedia.org/wiki/Marmion_(poem) [accessed 15 May 2014].

[11]Sisela Bok, *Lying: Moral Choice in Public and Private Life* (1978), quoted in BBC Ethics Guide http://www.bbc.co.uk/ethics/lying/lying_1.shtml.

are essential for healthy, well balanced personal, social and ethical development.[12] Sri Sathya Sai Baba says that 'The end of education is character' and the values of truth and right conduct go hand in hand in the development of one's character and place in society.[13]

Peace and contentment is gained when we learn to distinguish between 'needs' and 'wants'. With this understanding the urge to acquire more and more material possessions and the mental agitation caused in this pursuit gradually ceases and we are left feeling peaceful.[14]

When there is peace in the individual, there will be peace in the family. When there is peace in the family, there will be peace in the community. When there is peace in the community, there will be peace in the nation. When there is peace in the nation, there will be peace in the world.[15]

Love is a pure feeling from the heart. It is the power that rejoices at another's happiness and wishes for their well-being. It is a beneficial energy that flows through one's own body and mind enhancing one's health.

Non-violence is living in a way which causes as little harm as possible to oneself and others including animals, and the environment. It is a sign of a well-integrated, well-balanced personality. Such a person is in touch with an inner happiness which is part of one's real nature.

3.3 Legal Professional Ethics

The word 'ethics' is derived from the Greek work 'ethikos' meaning a system of rules of behaviour.[16] With respect to the legal profession the late Harun Hashim SCJ (as he then was) explained that it referred to the usages and customs in the legal profession involving the moral and professional duties of lawyers towards one another, to their clients and to the courts.[17] In fact before a law graduate can be admitted to the Bar as a 'qualified person' section 11 of the Malaysian *Legal Profession Act 1976* (LPA) specifies among other criteria that the applicant:

1. be of good character;
2. has not been convicted of any criminal offence whether in Malaysia or elsewhere that would render him unfit to be admitted to the profession;
3. has not been adjudicated a bankrupt;

[12] The British Institute of Sathya Sai education in Human Values F:\Conferences\Educare Conference 2014\Articles\British Institute of Sathya Sai Education.htm [accessed 15 April 2014].

[13] His Teachings, Educare http://www.srisathyasai.org.in/Pages/His_teachings/Educare.htm.

[14] Ibid.

[15] Ibid.

[16] Harun Hashim SCJ, 'Ethics in the Legal Profession: Now and in the Future' (1993) 2 *Malayan Law Journal* lxxxi.

[17] Ibid.

In Malaysia, legal ethics is a compulsory subject, taught to final year law students. Additionally all chambering students are required to attend an Ethics course run by the Bar Council. The ethics governing the legal profession have been embodied in the LPA 1976; *Legal Profession (Practice & Etiquette) Rules 1978* (LEPPER) and the *Legal Profession (Publicity) Rules 2001*(LEPUB) covering rules of conduct, etiquette, discipline and additional regulations of other dos and don'ts. They serve as a code of conduct to govern the legal profession. They are both prescriptive and disciplinary. These cover a wide spectrum of duties from the duty of a counsel to the court, to the client, to opposing counsel, the special duties of criminal lawyers and duty of counsel to society in general. The subject is taught in a comprehensive manner, by requiring a student to[18]:

- personally introspect, understand the relevant principles, issues and complexities of ethics;
- confront and resolve ethical dilemmas in practice;
- contemplate ethical conduct in the context of justice

The methodology adopted is pervasive, critical and problem- based with a practical approach as students undergo 12 weeks of legal attachment with either legal firms, the courts or the attorney general's chambers, where they are exposed to the practical challenges in the profession. They are also involved in serving the community in the legal aid centres, legal clinics, law awareness programmes and other civic activities.

Adrian Evans and Josephine Palermo (2009),[19] conducted an interesting study involving final year law students and young lawyers in a research exploring the relationship between values and ethical behavior for early career legal practitioners in Australia over the period between 2001 and 2003. A questionnaire comprising hypothetical ethical situations that could be faced by legal practitioners was distributed to final year law students in various Australian universities. The study tracked the participants from their final year in law school to the first three years of legal practice to study possible changes to their ethical decision making. Some of the questions posed to participants were whether they would:

1. be willing to take *pro bono* cases;
2. represent a corporation that was involved in unethical practices;
3. break a client confidentiality and report the client to relevant official departments;
4. not represent a friend;
5. report a nephew for cheating on a trust account;
6. not purchase shares based on insider information;

---

[18]Mariette Peters, *Legal Ethics in the Malaysian Legal Education System Quo Vadis...?* 25th Anniversary Special Commemorative Session 24–27, November 2005, Manila, Philippines https://www.scribd.com/document/61568568/Info-Lawyer-Ethics.

[19]Adrian Evans and Josephine Palermo, 'Lawyers and Ethics in Practice: The Impact of Clinical and Ethics Curricula on Lawyers' Ethical Decision-Making' (2007)1 *Alternative Law Journal* 12 https://ssrn.com/abstract=1349427.

In the first year of their study the results showed little difference between students who had taken the ethics course and those who hadn't. It was concluded that the responses mirrored the general ethical and moral values in society. In the second year of the study, the survey was conducted online and the responses were generally representative of the first year of the study. Over time it was seen that there was a decrease in willingness to take *pro bono* cases. This was attributed to the pressures of practice. Similar variations were observed in the responses to other situations over time. The authors note that though it could not be concluded whether such responses indicated more or less ethical behavior, the degree of consistency was nevertheless a guide to the 'flexibility or hardening of values over time'.[20] The authors conclude on the note that the results support a need for systematic continuous learning approaches to ethics education for legal practitioners.

3.4 The Duties of an Advocate and Solicitor

As a general rule an advocate and solicitor has a duty to uphold the interest of his client, the interest of justice and the dignity of the profession. He has at all times to be respectful and courteous to the court while fearlessly upholding the interests of his client, the interests of justice and the dignity of the profession without regard to any unpleasant consequences either to himself or to any other person. Advocates and solicitors are also prohibited from advertising their services although these rules have been relaxed to a certain extent. Nevertheless various complaints are made against lawyers by disgruntled clients from time to time and lawyers have been subjected to disciplinary proceedings by the Bar Council and suspended from practice or even struck off the roll. Section 77 LPA1976 empowers the Bar Council to regulate the professional practice, etiquette, conduct and discipline of advocates and solicitors.

3.4.1 Duty to the Court

Courts should be the bastions of truth that uphold justice. It is important that public confidence is not eroded. Counsel owes a higher duty to court than to his client. These include a duty to assist the court in finding the truth. In the event of a conflict of interest, a counsel's duty to court overrides his duty to his client.[21] As such counsel has a duty not to mislead the Court. He has to submit to the court all relevant facts, documents and authorities even where prejudicial to his client's case.[22] The Rulings of the Bar Council require Counsel to conduct with candour, courtesy and

---

[20] Ibid.

[21] Lord Alexander of Weedon QC, 'The Role of The Advocate in Our Society' (1992) 1 *Malayan Law Journal* xxxvii.

[22] *Legal Profession (Practice and Etiquette) Rules 1978* (Malaysia), rules 13–241.

fairness to court extending the same respect to witness and other counsel, including telephone calls, replies to correspondence, acceptance service of documents etc.[23] In *Dato' Wong GekMeng v Pathmanathan Mylvanam & Ors.*[24] Justice Adul Malik Ishak ruled that:

> the obligations of a solicitor towards his client are twofold, namely at equity, and at common law. At equity, the client-solicitor relationship is entirely fiduciary. This requires the solicitor to act with strict fairness &openness. At common law, the solicitor must act skilfully and carefully…But misconduct that will stir the court to life & that will receive the vehement disapproval of judges is deception. To practice deception in the court is akin to 'ridiculing' the court. That is misconduct so grave that words cannot describe it.

In *Cheah Cheng Hoc v PP,*[25] the Supreme Court reprimanded Counsel for concealment of documents affecting the credibility of a witness and misleading the court. In *Glebe Sugar Refining Company Limited v Trustees of the Ports and Harbours of Greenock* (1921) 37 TLR436, Viscount Finlay at the House of Lords severely chastised counsel for the lack of authorities submitted in a complex case:

> …this House expects and indeed insists that authorities which bear one way or the other upon matters under debate be brought to the attention of their Lordships by those who are aware of those authorities …quite irrespective of whether such authority assists the party which is so aware of it. It is an obligation of confidence between their Lordships and all those who assist in the debates in this House in the capacity of counsel.

Again, in *Re H Somapah Deceased,*[26] Aitken J had to admonish counsel for not citing a single authority or even a reference to text books to assist the court with regard to the law. Counsel has a duty to submit all relevant authorities even if it is against counsel's own client. In *Yap Ban Tick v Standard Chartered Bank,* [1995] 3 AMR 2580 the High Court similarly held that 'however tempting it may be, counsel should never suppress an adverse authority as to do so would mean that the legal profession would cease to enjoy the confidence of the State and democracy will perish'. The problem nevertheless continues to persist even in more modern times where internet searches and electronic sources are available. In *Copeland v Smith* [2000] 1WLR 1371 CA, Buxton LJ and Brooke LJ rebuked advocates who did not assist the court with relevant authorities and emphasised the obligation for advocates to keep themselves up to date with recent authorities.

There have been more serious breaches of professional duties committed by counsel than the mere failure to submit relevant authorities. In *Hoslan Hussin v. Majlis Agama Islam Wilayah Persekutuan, FC, Putrajaya* [2012] 4 CLJ 193, a lawyer threw his shoe at the Federal Court panel of judges, in anger and was sentenced to one year of imprisonment for contempt of court.

Re an Advocate & Solicitor [1962] MLJ 125, held that the preparation by a professional man of an affidavit that is untrue, and that is known to him to be untrue,

---

[23] See Bar Council Rulings 13–23.

[24] [1998] 1 [Malaysian] *Current Law Journal* 625.

[25] [1986] 1*Malayan Law Journal* 299 (SC).

[26] [1941] 1 LNS 67.

is a very serious offence. In *Rajasooria v Disciplinary Committee* [1955] MLJ 65, on the point of falsifying documents, the High Court held that even if there was no intention to deceive, the plain fact remains that the documents was a false document and might have deceived both the Registrar of Companies and the company itself, if the signatures of the 3 persons, who had recently ceased to be shareholders, had not been observed.

3.4.2 Duty to Client

Counsel has a duty to act fearlessly, to raise every issue, advance every argument and ask every question, however distasteful, which he thinks will help his client's case. He has to keep his client's disclosures confidential,[27] and advise him honestly.[28] Lord Denning quotes the conduct of Thomas Erskine,[29] who defended Tom Paine who was prosecuted for seditious libel for offensive remarks about King William III and King George I. In addressing the jury Erskine said "I will forever at all hazards assert the dignity, independence and integrity of the English Bar without which impartial justice, … can have no existence". The jury found Paine guilty and Erskine initially lost his position as Attorney General to the Prince of Wales. However he was later reappointed by the Prince, thereby vindicating the principle. As Prosecutors and defence counsel, lawyers have a duty to do justice by acting fairly and ensuring justice.[30]Apart from representing the best interests of the client, lawyers are trustees of their client's money and are accountable and responsible to their clients. Unfortunately, the old adage that "money is the root of all evil" finds its mark in the legal profession, as lawyers fall prey to greed and irresponsibility. Iin February 2019, an Atlanta lawyer Nathan Hardwick IV, was convicted of embezzling clients' money in the sum of USD 26.5 million. He was given a 15-year custodial sentence with six years of supervised release. Judge Eleanor Ross of the U.S. District Court for the Northern District of Georgia said:

> You are seriously a disappointment to our legal profession. I think your conduct in this case has been egregious—and not just as to your spending. It is indisputable that you were a greedy and deceitful person.[31]

Such dishonest lawyers abound all over the world. On 19 November 2018, a 37 year old Malaysian lawyer was charged with criminal breach of trust in the sum of

[27] *Tuckiar v The King* (1934) 52 CLR 335.

[28] *Legal Profession Act 1976* (LPA); *Legal Profession (Practice & Etiquette) Rules 1978*, rules 3–40.

[29] Lord Denning, n 1.

[30] *R v Banks* [1916] 2KB 621.

[31] Meredith Hobbs, 'Hardwick Sentenced to 15 Years for "Greedy and Deceitful" Conduct', *Daily Report* (12 February 2019) https://www.law.com/dailyreportonline/2019/02/12/hardwick-sentenced-to-15-years-for-greedy-and-deceitful-conduct/.

RM 100,000 due to his taxi driver client.[32] In *Tara Rajaratnam v Jaginder Singh and Suppiah*,[33] the plaintiff, had agreed to give her land to her brother-in-law as security for a loan. Instead what transpired was that the respondents, two lawyers, acting on the loan got her to sign certain allegedly loan documents which were in fact transfer documents of the land in favour of the 2nd. Respondent, who 18 days later transferred it to another Arul, who in turn transferred it to a development company under the 1st, respondent. The land was then sub-divided and sold to various purchasers. The respondents were convicted of fraud and Criminal Breach of Trust (CBT).

3.4.3 Duty to Fellow Lawyers

A lawyer shall at all times conduct himself with integrity and fairness. He should not engage in bickering in court,[34] or resort to delaying tactics. He should not cast unsubstantiated aspersions of dishonesty.[35] A lawyer should not appear as a witness if he is also acting as counsel for one of the parties.[36]

3.4.4 Duty to Society at Large

Lawyers have a duty to use their legal knowledge in furtherance of society's needs and not for purely personal materialistic benefits.[37] In this context some of the duties undertaken by lawyers include:

1. volunteering at the Legal Aid Centre to assist impecunious persons;
2. visits to those awaiting trial at the Sg. Buloh and Kajang Prison;
3. Dock brief clinic- pupils submit plea of mitigation to those on remand who plead guilty;
4. Legal Aid Clinic—free legal advice to the public whose household income is less than RM 2000 a month or RM 25,000 a year;
5. Juvenile Task Force—free legal assistance to children under remand in homes;
6. Duty to initiate law reform.

In 2012, the Malaysian Bar was conferred the United Nations (Malaysia) Award in recognition of the Malaysian Bar's continuous, courageous work in advancing

[32]Bernama, 'Lawyer Charged with CBT Involving more than 100 K' https://www.nst.com.my/news/crime-courts/2018/11/432658/lawyer-charged-cbt-involving-more-rm100k.

[33][1983] 2 *Malayan Law Journal*.

[34]*Beevis v Dawson* [1956] 3 All ER 837.

[35]*Clyne v New South Wales Bar Association* (1960) 104 CLR 186.

[36]*Legal Profession Act 1976* (LPA); *Legal Profession (Practice & Etiquette)Rules 1978*, rules 3–42.

[37]s 42(1)(g) LPA—object to protect and assist public in all matters, ancillary or incidental to the law.

Table 3.1 Comparative table of human values and legal professional ethics. *Source* The author

Value	Human value equivalent	Legal professional ethics
Truth	Honesty, trust, integrity, determination, fearlessness	Personal character—honesty, integrity. Higher duty owed to court. Duty to assist court in every manner even where prejudicial to client's case
Right conduct	Care of personal possessions, diet, hygiene, confidence, self reliance, good behaviour, helpful, not wasteful	Duty to—court, client, fellow lawyers, public and self. Integrity, fearlessness, courtesy, punctuality, confidentiality
Peace	Calm, focussed, contentment, dignity, humility, sense control, respect, understanding	Good relationship with all parties. Not to quarrel with- court, opposing lawyer, witness, client or public
Love	Acceptance, affection, compassion, thoughtfulness, service, sharing, forgiveness	Undertaking service to the public e.g. legal aid centre, free legal aid clinics, law reform, public awareness of laws, dock brief, visits to prisons and detention centres
Non-violence	Forbearance, morality, compassion, forgiveness, loyalty, good manners	Compliance to the rule of law, initiating law reform in a peaceful manner, educating public

the cause of democracy and human rights in Malaysia.[38] On the other hand, time and again lawyers have succumbed to greed and have been found guilty of criminal breach of trust, money laundering and other unprofessional indeed criminal activities,[39] which compelled the introduction of the compulsory ethics course as a prerequisite for every pupil aspiring to be admitted to the Malaysian Bar. The Course was initially introduced as a workshop but in July 2007, the Bar Council introduced the current Ethics and Professional Standards Course, combining the workshop with a compulsory written examination,[40] a reflection of the serious decline in values in the legal profession. At the same time looking at it from a positive view point it indicates the Malaysian Bar Council's commitment to rectify this decline and also to promote ethical values and practices among Malaysian lawyers (Table 3.1).

[38]The Malaysian Bar, 'The Malaysian Bar Presented UN Malaysia Award for its Pivotal Role in Malaysia's Democratic Development' (25 October 2012) http://www.malaysianbar.org.my/bar_news/berita_badan_peguam/the_malaysian_bar_presented_un_malaysia_award_for_its_pivotal_role_in_malaysias_democratic_development.html.

[39]See Bar Council Reports on Disciplinary Matters http://www.malaysianbar.org.my/disciplinary_orders/disciplinary_orders_december_2018.html Accessed on 10 Feb. 2019.

[40]Bar Council Ethics & Professional Standards Course for Pupils (18 and 19 Nov 2009) http://www.malaysianbar.org.my/bar_news/berita_badan_peguam/bar_council_ethics_professional_standards_course_for_pupils_18_and_19_nov_2009.html.

3.5 Conclusion

A commitment to legal ethics involves a commitment to basic human values. The values promoted in SSE are suitable for all stages of life and every walk of life. The planting of moral values or human values cannot be over-emphasised. All cultures bear testament to moral stories introduced from early childhood. These have to be nurtured at every stage of human life and translated into daily activities at home, in society and every professional organisation. Lawyers are uniquely responsible for upholding the law which is founded on principles of justice, fairness and equity. Ethical responsibility, duty and integrity are an inherent part of the legal profession and have been enshrined in the *Legal Profession Act 1976*. It is further reinforced by incorporating them into the curriculum of Law Faculties and the activities carried out by law students in Malaysia, to help mould them into responsible and ethical professionals. However the mere passing of mandatory ethics courses will not produce an ethical profession. It will at best serve as a constant reminder. Real values spring from the heart that has been nurtured from young and carried into adulthood exhibited in daily living.

Bibliography

Articles

Bok, Sisela, *Lying: Moral Choice in Public and Private Life* (1978) quoted in BBC Ethics Guide http://www.bbc.co.uk/ethics/lying/lying_1.shtml

Delors, Jacques, 'Learning: The Treasure Within; Report to UNESCO of the International Commission on Education for the Twenty-first Century (highlights)' (UNESCO Publishing, 1996) https://unesdoc.unesco.org/ark:/48223/pf0000109590

Dhall, Pal, *Sathya Sai Primary School Murwillumbah Annual Report 2009* http://www.sathyasai.org/education/supreme-end-of-education

Evans, Adrian and Josephine Palermo, 'Lawyers and Ethics in Practice: The Impact of Clinical and Ethics Curricula on Lawyers' Ethical Decision-Making' (2007)1 *Alternative Law Journal* 112

Halstead, J. Mark and Monica J. Taylor, 'Learning and Teaching about Values: A Review of Recent Research' (2000) 30(2) *Cambridge Journal of Education* 169

Hashim, Harun, *Ethics in the Legal Profession: Now and in the Future* [1993] 2 *Malayan Law Journal* lxxxi

Hobbs, Meredith, 'Hardwick Sentenced to 15 Years for "Greedy and Deceitful" Conduct', *Daily Report* (12 February 2019) https://www.law.com/dailyreportonline/2019/02/12/hardwick-sentenced-to-15-years-for-greedy-and-deceitful-conduct/

Lakshmi, J., 'Innovative and Best Practices in Teaching of Value Education' (2014) 2(5) *Tactful Management Research Journal* 1 http://oldtm.lbp.world/UploadedArticles/125.pdf

Lord Alexander of Weedon QC, 'The Role of The Advocate in Our Society' [1992] 1 *Malayan Law Journal* xxxvii

Lord Denning, 'The Honest Lawyer' (1983) 2 *Current Law Journal* 174

Peters, Mariette, *Legal Ethics in the Malaysian Legal Education System Quo Vadis…?*, 25th Anniversary Special Commemorative Session 24–27, November 2005, Manila, Philippines https://docuri.com/download/info-lawyer-ethics-_59a7cd10f58171db1d42d608_pdf

Sir Walter Scott, *Marmion* (1808)Canto VI, Stanza 17 http://en.wikipedia.org/wiki/Marmion_(poem)

Statutes

Legal Profession (Practice & Etiquette) Rules 1978
Legal Profession Act 1976 (LPA) 1976

Cases

Beevis v Dawson [1956] 3 All ER 837
Cheah Cheng Hoc v PP [1986] 1 MLJ 299 SC
Clyne v New South Wales Bar Association (1960) 104 CLR 186
Copeland v Smith [2000] 1WLR 1371 CA
Dato' Wong GekMeng v PathmanathanMylvanam&Ors[1998] 1 CLJ 625
Glebe Sugar Refining Company Limited v Trustees of the Ports and Harbours of Greenock (1921) 37 TLR436
HoslanHussin v. Majlis Agama Islam Wilayah Persekutuan, FC, Putrajaya [2012] 4 CLJ 193
R v Banks [1916] 2 KB 621
Rajasooria v Disciplinary Committee [1955] MLJ 65
Re an Advocate & Solicitor [1962] MLJ 125
Re H Somapah Deceased [1941] 1 LNS 67
Tara Rajaretnam v Jaginder Singh and Suppiah[1983] 2 MLJ
Tuckiar v The King (1934) 52 CLR 335
Yap Ban Tick v Standard Chartered Bank, [1995] 3 AMR 2580

Others

Bar Council Ethics & Professional Standards Course for Pupils (18 and 19 Nov 2009) http://www.malaysianbar.org.my/bar_news/berita_badan_peguam/bar_council_ethics_professional_standards_course_for_pupils_18_and_19_nov_2009.html
Bar Council Rulings 13–23
His Teachings, Educare http://www.srisathyasai.org.in/Pages/His_teachings/Educare.htm
Lexico.com http://www.oxforddictionaries.com/definition/english/education
Sri Sathya Sai Baba, *Sri Sathya Sai University* (2007) 103 http://www.sathyasai.org/files2007/globaloverview/chapter5_30jun07.pdf
The American Heritage Dictionary of the English Language (Houghton Mifflin Company, 4th ed, 2009) http://www.thefreedictionary.com/education
The British Institute of Sathya Sai Education in Human Values F:\Conferences\Educare Conference 2014\Articles\British Institute of Sathya Sai Education.htm
The Malaysian Bar, 'The Malaysian Bar presented UN Malaysia Award for its Pivotal Role in Malaysia's Democratic Development' (25 October 2012) http://www.malaysianbar.org.my/bar_news/berita_badan_peguam/the_malaysian_bar_presented_un_malaysia_award_for_its_pivotal_role_in_malaysias_democratic_development.html

Chapter 4
Teaching Law Undercover

Stewart Manley

Abstract This chapter describes my experience from 2006 to 2012 teaching law surreptitiously to refugees and young activists on the Thailand-Myanmar border. Education was a way for my colleagues and students to escape—if not physically, at least in their minds—the danger, powerlessness and living conditions of the border. Education was a secret gate in the barbed wire fence. It kindled their hopes for a brighter future. Without romanticizing their situation, I attempt to capture their resilience, courage and good cheer. I then place the experience in the context of my more recent teaching positions in Malaysia, explaining how teaching helps me maintain perspective and prompts me to view legal education as ultimately a social human enterprise.

Keywords Legal education · Refugees · Human rights practice · Human rights perspective · Myanmar and Malaysia education compared

4.1 Undercover

The swish-swishing breeze found its way through the maze of bamboo stalks. I looked up the slippery, muddy incline. Another 30 m and I would arrive. I looked down. One foot was stuck deep in the mud, the other precariously close to sinking. Laughing and chatter made me turn. With dismay, I saw my students in their bright shirts and dresses—hand-woven in striped and chequered patterns from deep purple, aqua blue, glowing pink, and cherry red yarns—nimbly hopping on rubber slippers from dry spot to rock and back again up the hill. 'I still have a lot to learn,' I thought, as a cheerful student mercifully reached out to extricate me.

It was the rainy season again in Mae La Refugee Camp—the largest of Thailand's refugee settlements, nestled among misty granite cliffs along the country's remote

Mr. Stewart Manley, Lecturer, Faculty of Law, University of Malaya, Kuala Lumpur, Malaysia. Email: stewart.manley@um.edu.my.

M. Zan (ed.), *Legal Education and Legal Traditions: Selected Essays*,
SpringerBriefs in Environment, Security, Development and Peace,
https://doi.org/10.1007/978-3-030-50903-3_4

border with Myanmar.[1] The camp served—and continues to serve—as a repository for what had been until a few years ago, a regular flow of civilians fleeing the decades-long armed conflict between the Myanmar government and ethnic rebel groups. Undocumented and with few to no belongings, refugees do not pass through immigration checkpoints with passports and visas. Instead, they cross over rivers and through remote jungle valleys. Some of these were my law students.

The school where I taught, called the Leadership and Management Course (though it was called a course, it was a school), was located in a relatively isolated area of what is called 'Zone B' of the camp.[2] Public transportation from the nearest city—a pickup truck with two benches in the back called a *songthaew* (literally, 'two rows')—let me off at the side of the main road after passing through several police and military checkpoints. I would give a brief smile to the Thai soldier at the camp gate that was confident enough to show that I knew where I was going, but subtle enough not to alert him to the fact that I was not officially permitted to enter.

Down a hill, through the grounds of a high school, and I was passing by a hand-operated water pump on my right that was constantly in use, as young men and women filled buckets with fresh well water to carry home for cooking and washing. On my left up a slight slope was a barbershop populated with men with little to do but smoke cigarettes and chew betel quids—packets of areca nut and tobacco wrapped in betel leaf, a mild stimulant, and lined with slaked lime to help absorption. I tried it once and it reminded me of the moments after the dentist injected novocaine into my gums. The path then took me by a primary school on my left where bamboo huts were packed with children repeating over and over in English, 'Hello, how are you? Hello, how are you?' These three scenes that I passed every morning on my way to class—camp residents struggling through the daily difficulties of living in primitive conditions, men sitting idly without jobs and a new generation striving to become better-educated—embodied life in the camp and reflected the frustrations and hopes of the camp residents.

My school was a product of those aspirations. Most young adults in the camp had two options: stay home or go to school. Many chose, or perhaps were forced by their parents, to attend one of the several post-secondary institutions scattered throughout the camp. Rampant unemployment largely resulted from the lack of businesses in the camp that were large enough to hire anyone other than family members. The marketplace had a number of vendors selling vegetables, meats, clothes and wares, but there was no industry to employ the thousands of adults who needed jobs. The barbed wire surrounding the camp ensured that. The United Nations and a host of nongovernmental organizations provided rice, salt, other staples and basic healthcare, obviating in part the need for money to buy basic necessities.[3] These organizations

[1]George Kent, 'The Nutrition of Refugees', in Doreen Elliott and Uma A. Segal (eds), *Refugees Worldwide: Volume 1: Global Perspectives* (Praeger 2012) 113, 118.

[2]For an overview of camp governance, see Suwattana Thadaniti and Supang Chantavanich (eds), *The Impact of Displaced People's Temporary Shelters on Their Surrounding Environment* (Springer 2014) 169.

[3]Mac McClelland, *For Us Surrender Is Out of the Question: A Story from Burma's Never-Ending War* (Soft Skull Press 2010) 204.

for the most part hired foreigners and Thai nationals, although exceptions were made for some of the manual labour positions.

Lecturing to a class that included students who had difficulty sometimes holding basic conversations in English taught me about how to teach law. I had to be able to articulate the 'macro' aspects of law. For instance, if I was discussing criminal law, I had to be able to explain how the people of a country, through their government, determined that certain acts endangered the security and well-being of their society, and that criminal law establishes what aspires to be a fair and transparent way of deterring those who would commit, and punishing those who have committed, those acts. In contract law, I needed to be able to convey to my students that, unfortunately, people do not always fulfil their promises, and that contract law helps hold people to those promises and provides remedies when a contract is breached. These concepts are obvious to lawyers and students schooled in law, but are not so evident to young adults who have spent much of their lives farming or hunting.

Yet while the students of LMC may have lacked English language skills and worldly wherewithal, they had front row seats to living conditions and experiences that made the rule of law urgently relevant to their lives. Imagine, for a moment, teaching the basics of refugee law to refugees. There is probably no one in the world who would be more interested (or amused). Or teaching human rights law to people who had fled government abuse and now lived in a community whose gates were guarded by armed soldiers. Thus, while perhaps I opened their eyes to laws that they had no inkling existed, they also opened my eyes with personal vignettes of how in the corners of the world, in the looted homes of rural villages or the fields burned by a departing army, the laws were nice to hear about but for them remained as fictional as the Hollywood movies they so enjoyed watching.

My second 'undercover' teaching job was located two hours to the south of Mae La Camp, in a pleasant Thai village dotted with tamarind and mango trees and surrounded by rice paddies. With a driveway bordered by huge palms acting as sentinels and three scruffy dogs running out to greet visitors, the small complex of green-roofed structures neighboured by a pond sprouting violet and white lotus flowers looked like any typical rural Thai house.

This was intentional. The school's location and curriculum were for the most part closely-guarded secrets. To the Thai villagers who would pass by, deliver the drinking water or fish in the pond, the Peace Law Academy was merely a school for migrants. Without the sanction of the Thai government, at least during its initial years, the school maintained a low profile and the students remained at risk of arrest by police or immigration officers. Their safety and anonymity were of paramount concern.

Funded largely by American, Swedish and Japanese organizations, the Academy's objective was not so much to train opponents of the Myanmar military government as it was to capacitate budding leaders from the country's various states and divisions to promote and protect the rule of law. The quality of legal education in Myanmar had suffered under military rule[4] and even the students with law degrees readily told me that they had barely learned anything. After graduating in two years, it was hoped that they would return to their cities and villages to take up community leadership positions and train others in human rights and law. In this way, the values underlying all the Academy's courses—equality, respect, transparency, good governance, fairness and justice—would be shared throughout the country.[5] These are the types of values in legal education that are, arguably, crucial to systemic justice and the integrity of the globalising legal community.[6]

The students in the Peace Law Academy, for the most part, had experienced a different side of the Myanmar military government's reign from those in the camp. For nearly fifty years, the people of Myanmar had been—and some would argue continue to be—largely deprived of basic freedoms and rights by the ruling military regime (although no longer technically in power, the constitution of Myanmar reserves one-quarter of seats in both the Union and the 14 State and Division Legislatures for military officials directly appointed by the Commander-in-Chief).[7] Thus, in contrast to the students in the camp who had experienced the impact of actual warfare, most of those in the Academy were acutely aware of the more subtle oppression brought about by government abuses and restrictions.

Probably the most dramatic example of the military flexing its muscle during my tenure working for the Academy and its administrative organization, the Burma Lawyers' Council, was during a May 2009 conference in Bangkok on criminal accountability for Myanmar's then military leaders. A wide variety of international human rights organizations and Burmese advocates met to discuss a potential international inquiry into allegations of crimes against humanity and war crimes in Myanmar. Giving me a jolt of excitement and that odd surreal feeling when real danger appears, rumours circulated that the Thai and Myanmar governments had sent agents to infiltrate the meetings. The Myanmar government had apparently issued an arrest warrant for the General Secretary of the Burma Lawyers' Council and was reportedly trying to either kidnap or kill him.[8] This was a man with whom I had eaten many meals and—please do not spread this—I accidentally locked inside a Bangkok office for several hours. To add to the tension, security personnel advised us to eat our meals in a sheltered inner area of the dining room of the hotel. Fortunately, while my mind was

---

[4]Myint Zan, 'Legal Education in Burma since the Mid-1960s' (2008) 12 *Journal of Burma Studies* 63.

[5]For an overview of the Academy, see Burma Lawyers' Council, 'Opening Ceremony of Advanced Internship Program in Human Rights and Law' (2009) 32 *LawKaPaLa: Legal Journal on Burma* 14–16.

[6]Josephine Palermo and Adrian Evans, 'Australian Law Students' Values: How They Impact on Ethical Behaviour' (2005) 15(1 & 2) *Legal Education Review* 4.

[7]Constitution of the Republic of the Union of Myanmar 2008 (English translation) arts 109(b), 141(b).

[8]Dan Withers, 'Aung Htoo, BLC: "Than Shwe Fears the ICC"', *Democratic Voice of Burma* (online at 22 October 2010) http://english.dvb.no/interview/aung-htoo-blc-%E2%80%98than-shwe-fears-the-icc%E2%80%99/12370; Andrew Marshall, 'Putting Burma's Junta on Trial', *Time* (online at 7 August 2009) http://content.time.com/time/world/article/0,8599,1915174,00.html.

still in a fog of exhilaration and fear, clearer-minded activists spirited the General Secretary to an anonymous hotel room, where he went into hiding and later left the country to seek asylum.

This was the first time (and fortunately so far has been the last) that I felt a small fraction of the sensation that so many of my Burmese colleagues felt of being targeted by a powerful government. The truth was, of course, that I was not the target and I was never in any real danger. Yet there was uncertainty and foreboding in the air of that conference room. This gave me a glimpse of what the Academy students must have felt when they passed through a police checkpoint on the way to the market, or when a Thai soldier suddenly appeared in the doorway during one of my lectures, wondering what we were doing.

I may have taught undercover, but for me it was for the most part an adventure. The risk I faced—possible but unlikely deportation—paled in comparison to those of the Myanmar students, teachers, lawyers, doctors, politicians and others from every walk of life who laboured—often in silence, for almost no pay—to bring better days to their country. Each of them could have easily given up. Many could have resettled to more prosperous countries and forgotten about their homeland. Others could have abandoned their dreams of a brighter future in exchange for a stop to government harassment and, in some cases, detention. They did not, and in their resilience, they taught me lessons about courage and strength. There is some irony, therefore, in the title of this piece. For although people called me 'teacher', *sayar* (Burmese) or *th'ra* (Karen), I hope that at least some of them took pleasure in knowing that 'student' was the more appropriate word.

4.2 Out from Cover

Beginning in around 2012, improvements in the political conditions in Myanmar brought about a number of changes that affected many lives, including mine. Most of my colleagues felt safe enough to return to Myanmar. The Peace Law Academy continued for another session but then also moved inside Myanmar. Efforts to repatriate refugee camp residents have increased (although distrust in the Myanmar government continues).[9] A significant portion of the international funding moved on or dried up.[10] I also moved on. I contacted Professor Dr. Myint Zan, the editor of this book, who suggested that I apply for a position at the Faculty of Law of Multimedia University in Melaka (Malacca), Malaysia. Fortunately, I was offered a post and I worked there from 2012 to 2014. I currently teach at the Faculty of Law of the University of Malaya in Kuala Lumpur.

[9] Ron Corben, 'Myanmar Refugees in Thai Camps Face Repatriation Challenges', *VOA News* (online at 11 May 2017) https://www.voanews.com/a/myanmar-refugees-thai-camps-repatriation-challenges/3847329.html.

[10] Saw Yan Naing, 'Left Behind: Karen Refugees at Mae La Camp', *The Irrawaddy* (online at 28 April 2017) https://reliefweb.int/report/thailand/left-behind-karen-refugees-mae-la-camp.

As I transitioned from the Thailand-Myanmar border to urban Malaysia, from grassroots human rights work to university life, from dusty refugee camp paths to skyscraper-lined highways, and from undercover to out from cover, I came to understand that perhaps the most enduring gift from my experience teaching law on the border is perspective. It is a well from which I draw from time to time. When traffic on the way to work is bad, I look at my new car and remember slowly riding a bicycle to the Peace Law Academy in the hot sun. When the air conditioning in a classroom seems sluggish, I remind myself of how the bamboo structures in Mae La Camp were built with permanent openings to let the breeze in.

Perspective is not, however, only about being able to appreciate comfort, stability or even intellectual and material wealth; perspective is also about understanding how opportunity enables, and in this regard I have been truly fortunate. To some extent—through our attitude, drive and effort—we make our own opportunities, but I am convinced that circumstances outside my control—my citizenship, my native language, my parents' emphasis on education—largely contributed to opening a wide range of opportunities for travel, work and study. I hope that the young men in the barbershop, and the children memorizing English expressions, and the Peace Law Academy students, can find their way to meaningful and rewarding opportunity. Some of them surely will, hopefully all, but their path is not an easy one. Many doors that were open for me will be closed for them. It is in mitigating the inequity of opportunity, I believe, that education has perhaps its greatest potential.

Perspective for me also means appreciating how all of us—regardless of our backgrounds—need encouragement in education. In the eyes of my Malaysian students, I can see the hopes, fears and uncertainties that I saw in my Myanmar students. Though perhaps different, their concerns are just as urgent and important. As older adults, many of us probably look back to our student life as 'the good ol' days', but if we are honest, we should recognize that being a student is not easy. I remember fearing one of my classes with all my soul—there were only 6 of us, and I knew that the teacher would call on me to participate. When contemplating getting a job after graduation, I recall the helplessness I felt in the face of what seemed like monumental political and economic forces beyond my control. As teachers, our ability to affect these factors is limited, but we can help our students face them with hope and confidence. Recently during my Mooting class, I was particularly impressed with the oral submissions of a few of my Malaysian students. They had prepared well, they were brave but measured in their positions, and they spoke with passion. During the feedback session afterwards, I could see that my praise for them was not just words, but energy. Positive energy that filled them with strength and promise.

Ultimately, in legal education, we do the best we can for our students given the environment in which we operate. I believe that what we do is a human endeavour, in which our final goal must be a human one. To improve our lot as we travel through the challenges of living together in society. To gradually, but without hesitation, move away from historical abuses and injustices to a fairer, more peaceful and more equitable place in time. Teaching on the border and in Malaysia has taught me this. Sometimes I imagine my Myanmar students, perhaps working with disenfranchised labourers in a remote village or holding a UN workshop in a bustling Yangon conference room. I imagine my Malaysian students, advocating for freedom of speech and association or, perhaps one day, issuing opinions from the Malaysian judicial bench. All of them, equally, are bringing about the justice that I dreamed of when I decided to attend law school in 1998 and when I decided, back in 2006, to leave a private law firm in Phoenix, Arizona to teach law undercover.

Bibliography

Books

Kent, George, 'The Nutrition of Refugees', in Doreen Elliott and Uma A. Segal (eds), *Refugees Worldwide: Volume 1: Global Perspectives* (Praeger 2012) 113

McClelland, Mac, *For Us Surrender Is Out of the Question: A Story from Burma's Never-Ending War* (Soft Skull Press 2010) 204

Suwattana Thadaniti and Supang Chantavanich (eds), *The Impact of Displaced People's Temporary Shelters on Their Surrounding Environment* (Springer 2014) 169

Articles

Burma Lawyers' Council, 'Opening Ceremony of Advanced Internship Program in Human Rights and Law' (2009) 32 *LawKaPaLa: Legal Journal on Burma* 14

Corben, Ron, 'Myanmar Refugees in Thai Camps Face Repatriation Challenges', *VOA News* (online at 11 May 2017) https://www.voanews.com/a/myanmar-refugees-thai-camps-repatriation-challenges/3847329.html

Myint Zan, 'Legal Education in Burma since the Mid-1960s' (2008) 12 *Journal of Burma Studies* 63

Palermo, Josephine and Adrian Evans, 'Australian Law Students' Values: How They Impact on Ethical Behaviour' (2005) 15(1 & 2) *Legal Education Review* 4

Saw Yan Naing, 'Left Behind: Karen Refugees at Mae La Camp', *The Irrawaddy* (online at 28 April 2017) https://reliefweb.int/report/thailand/left-behind-karen-refugees-mae-la-camp

Other

Constitution of the Republic of the Union of Myanmar 2008 (English translation)

Part II
Legal and Philosophical Traditions

Chapter 5
Socrates' Refusal to Escape from Prison: Later Philosophers' Possible Views on the *Crito*

Charlene Constance Chai and Myint Zan

Abstract This chapter analyses what subsequent philosophers would have commented on some of the reasons given in Plato's *Crito* as to why Socrates should not escape from prison. Philosophers post Plato/Socrates views pertaining to what can be considered political theory concerning 'obligation to obey the law' are briefly canvassed and what these philosophers might have commented on the reasons given in the *Crito* is stated. Arguments given in the *Crito* is commented from the viewpoints of Aristotle, Thomas Hobbes, John Locke, Jean Jacques Rousseau, H. L. A. Hart and Lon Fuller. While we are unsure of what Aristotle and Rousseau might have said on the reasons given in the *Crito* we propose that while Hobbes, and H. L. A. Hart might approve of the reasons Locke and Fuller probably might not agree with them.

Keywords Aristotle and 'sinning against philosophy' · Thomas Hobbes and 'obeying the sovereign' · John Locke and 'right of revolution' · Jean Jacques Rousseau and 'general will' · H. L. A. Hart and 'rule of recognition' · Lon Fuller and 'morality of law'

5.1 Introduction: The *Crito*

Plato, 428–348 BC, one of ancient Greece's great philosophers, was also a student of Socrates.[1] Socrates wrote nothing during his life time, however Plato immortalized him by writing a philosophical dialogue where Socrates was the major character and one of them is the *Crito*.[2] In the *Crito* by Plato, the dialogue between Socrates' friend Crito and Socrates which took place in Socrates' prison cell portrayed the character

Charlene Constance Chai, LLB, law firm of Kuek, Ong and Associates, Petaling Jaya, Malaysia. Email: Charlene.chai.91@gmail.com and Myint Zan. Email: myintzan@yahoo.com.au.

[1]Biography.com, *Plato*, (Web page, 2015) http://www.biography.com/people/plato-9442588.

[2]Excerpt from *The Concise Columbia Encyclopedia*, 'Plato: Founder of the Academy' (Columbia University Press, 1991).

M. Zan (ed.), *Legal Education and Legal Traditions: Selected Essays*, SpringerBriefs in Environment, Security, Development and Peace,
https://doi.org/10.1007/978-3-030-50903-3_5

of Socrates particularly as a citizen who had been unjustly condemned but willing to face punishment meted out to him obeying the laws of the state of Athens. The *Crito* was set in the 399 BC[3] during which in Athens, society and its state exist based on a social contract.[4] Athenians were bound to follow its laws. One of the Athenian laws prescribed the offence against the desecration of the sacred,[5] and in which the Jury have the power to choose either one of the punishments proposed by both the prosecution and the defendant.[6]

Socrates had been put on trial on the charge of failing to acknowledge the gods that the city acknowledges and for corrupting the mind of the youths. At the end of the trial the jury voted for the prosecution's proposal of death by a margin for conviction of 360–140 for Socrates' alleged offences.[7] The conversation which took place revolved around the notion of justice and injustice in which both of them, initially, held divergent opinions. Crito urged Socrates to escape as he believed that Socrates had been unjustly penalised. His reasoning suggested that it would be unjust for Socrates to remain in prison and succumb to the punishment of his enemies as it would bring greater injustice to his sons, who would then be without a father.[8]

Socrates categorically refused to take up his friend Crito's offer and provided several arguments as to why he must remain in prison and face punishment. Among others, Socrates asserted that if he were to escape from prison it would be tantamount to repaying injustice with injustice.[9] He contended that Crito's argument merely reflects the "opinion of many". In contrast he, Socrates, opined that his decision should be based on the views of someone who is an expert, which can arguably be said that Socrates was referring to himself as 'the expert' to which Crito should listen. Socrates then elucidated that Athenian laws – which actually materialised and spoke to him. Socrates quoted 'The Laws' as speaking to him – to obey 'them' and the decision reached by the jury. He explained there was a 'social contract' between the State and its citizens a form of social contract in which to ensure 'self-preservation' (and the State's preservation) it is the obligation of the citizens to obey the State's or the Ruler's law unconditionally.

In the *Crito* 'The Laws' and Socrates seemed to have at least implicitly agreed that it was the 'laws' of Athens which brought about his existence wherein it allows his parents to marry thus making him legitimate and later allowing Socrates himself to be married. These are only a few among many other benefits the Athenian laws have provided Socrates, 'The Laws' argued. Echoing (or) following 'The Laws' Socrates

[3]See generally Plato, *Crito*, translated by Benjamin Jowett (C. Scribner's Sons, 1871).

[4]Ibid.

[5]Jakub Filonik, 'Athenian Laws on Impiety: Some notes on the Procedures' (2012) Proceedings of the International Web Conference conducted by the Centre for Classical Studies http://antik-yar.ru/events-2/ancient-civilization-political-institutions-and-legal-regulation/filonik-j?lang=en.

[6]David D Philips, *The Law of Ancient Athens* (University of Michigan Press, 2013).

[7]University of Missouri-Kansas City School of Law, *Criminal Procedure in Ancient Greece and the Trial of Socrates* http://law2.umkc.edu/faculty/projects/ftrials/socrates/greekcrimpro.html.

[8]Ibid. 4.

[9]Ibid.

all but stated that however oppressive and prejudicial the laws were they are based on the social contract as explained above and that he should observe the Athenian Laws since going against them is to do injustice and bring great harm to the State. Again, endorsing what 'The Laws' asserted, Socrates said no citizen was forced to accept the social contract and since they can either choose to leave (if they be dissatisfied with the laws) after becoming aware of them or trying to change them. Echoing the laws Socrates stated that he had agreed to abide by the law and undertake the punishment it meted out to him through operation of those laws.

The remaining part of this chapter will discuss mainly the social contract argument and 'repaying injustice with injustice' argument stated above by Socrates' as narrated by Plato in the *Crito* with the views of a few jurists who 'flourished' after Socrates. What the later philosophers and jurists would have said about Socrates' argument based on the writers 'understanding and application of these philosophers' and jurists' views that can be discerned in their philosophies.

5.2 Aristotle

Aristotle, 384–322 BC, one of the most notable Western philosophers, was a student of Plato, who was the pupil of Socrates, and teacher of Alexander the Great.[10] Aristotle was very influential especially in the Middle Ages. Aristotle was born in 384 BC, in Stagira, a Greek village on the Chalcidice peninsula which forms part of the region of Central Macedonia. Aristotle's ancestors were believed to be the physicians of the Macedonian royal family for several generations.[11] When Aristotle was seventeen, he was sent to study at Plato's Academy in Athens, where he remained for twenty years until the death of Plato in 347 BC.[12] He was later invited by King Amyntas', King of Macedonian, to tutor his son, Alexander, who would then be 'Alexander the Great', for five years until King Amyntas died leaving Alexander in power.[13]

During 335 BC Aristotle went back to Athens and founded his own school, which he ran for twelve years. In the 323 BC Alexander the Great died and the government of Athens was overthrown by anti-Macedonian forces and they declared war against Alexander's successor. Having a close connection with the Macedonian royal family, Aristotle was associated with the Macedonians and was considered to be anti-Athenian and Pro-Macedonian, hence leaving him unpopular with the ruling power. The ruling power was on the brink of arresting Aristotle and brought charges of

---

[10] Stanford Encyclopedia of Philosophy, *Aristotle's Political Theory* (1998) http://plato.stanford.edu/entries/aristotle-politics/.

[11] Biography.com, *Aristotle* (Web page, 2015) http://www.biography.com/people/aristotle-9188415.

[12] Ibid.

[13] Ibid.

impiety against him, but he fled to his country house in Chalcis to escape his prosecution. Aristotle claimed that he fled so that "Athenians might not have another opportunity of sinning against philosophy as they already had done in the person of Socrates."[14] A year later, in 322 BC Aristotle died of a digestive ailment.

Aristotle's fate at the end of his life, has had one similarity with that of Socrates, in that while sojourning at the city of Athens both of them became involved or entangled with charges of 'impiety' which was punishable by death. However, first, unlike Socrates, Aristotle was not formally charged with 'impiety if 'charge' means Aristotle had had his day in court which he never had. In contrast Socrates had his day in Court for Socrates' trial was over in a day. Aristotle was not charged as yet when he chose to escape what is believed to be a persecution.[15] It can be clearly seen that Aristotle would view Socrates' indictment as something that is unjust. He claimed that Athens had '...*sinned*...' against philosophy in sentencing Socrates to death.

Aristotle's decision to justify his escape may be largely influenced by his view regarding natural law theory. Aristotle holds the belief that law is the study that has a '*telos*' which means a purpose towards an end it is served.[16] He put forth that natural law ought to be something which moves towards a certain goal or end, which is to achieve happiness. An act or law is deemed good or bad is dependent on whether it contributes to or deters us from our proper human end. Aristotle and his followers believed that this '*telos*' is understood in terms of completion, perfection and well-being. Therefore, achieving happiness requires a wide range of intellectual and moral virtues that enable us to understand the nature of happiness and motivate us to seek it in a reliable and consistent way.

Hence, law should support virtuous existence, advancement of lives of individuals and promote the perfect community. From this it can be concluded that Aristotle would see the laws of Athens in prosecuting (and in a few senses persecuting) both Socrates and himself as an injustice as it goes against his notion of what is deemed to be the natural law. As such, his escape is justified since for Socrates was to have faced punishment based on an unjust law. Would Aristotle have approved of Socrates' reasons for non-escape? Aristotle believed It was unjust that Socrates have been prosecuted and punished. This is discernible from Aristotle's statement that (Aristotle) would not allow Athens to sin again against philosophy.

In quite a few aspects of their philosophies Aristotle's views diverged from that of his former teacher Plato. Would Aristotle have stated that Socrates should have listened to advice of his friend Crito? Compared to the naïve or at least simple-minded Crito, Aristotle's power of thinking and rhetoric is far more formidable. It would have been interesting to envisage (only) what counter-arguments would Aristotle have proffered to Socrates and indeed 'The Laws' but in a 'counter-factual hypothetical'

---

[14]Nicholas Fearn, *Zeno and the Tortoise* (Atlantic Books, 2001) ch 6, p 2.

[15]Leo Strauss, *Persecution and the Art of Writing* (University of Chicago Press, 2013) 85.

[16]Liesbeth Huppes-Cluysenaer and Coelho, Nuno MMS (eds), *Aristotle and the Philosophy of Law: Theory, Practice and Justice* (Springer, 2013) 116.

if the hypothetical Aristotle instead of the actual Crito has succeed in arguing Socrates to escape then this academic exercise would not have been necessary.

5.3 Thomas Hobbes

Thomas Hobbes, 1588–1679, was an English philosopher, who in his most famous work *The Leviathan* (1651) had presented and argued his social contract theory,[17] which became the foundation of most Western political philosophy.[18] In moral and political philosophy, this social contract theory addresses the origin of the society and the legitimacy of the authority of the state over its individual; it is the view that a person's moral and political obligations are dependent upon the contract or agreement among themselves and also the Ruler.

Hobbes' hypothesis of the State of Nature, prior to the existence of the social contract is that the natural condition of the people and society are essentially equal, physically and mentally, in which it placed every individual at the same level in the struggle to survive. This leads to the three main natural causes to quarrel among people, which are the competition for limited supplies of material possessions, the distrust amongst one another and also hostility among people to retain power and reputation. This State of Nature of humans is a state of perpetual war of all against all, where nothing is unjust. Hobbes' social contract theory is driven by the desire of its people to live adequately thus to rise above this state through the social contract.[19]

Under Hobbes' social contract theory, in justifying political obligation, he reasoned it by claiming that men are naturally self-interested, yet they are rational.[20] He believed that in return for security provided by the State or Ruler and to be able to live in a civil society they will choose to submit to the authority of the sovereign.[21] Therefore this State of Nature of wanting to preserve life ought to be the greatest lesson of the natural law. This natural law commands each man to be willing to pursue peace while retaining the right to continue to pursue war when peace fails. In rationalising this, men constructed a social contract in which they must agree to establish a society by collectively surrendering all their rights and freedoms against one another to some authority that would then enforce this contract.[22]

Hobbes' theory of social contract seems to suggest that to ensure peace and self-perseverance the state and its citizens must both agree to live under common

---

[17] Thomas Hobbes, *The Leviathan* (1651) ch XIII.

[18] Stanford Encyclopedia of Philosophy, *Hobbes's Moral and Political Philosophy* (Web page, 2002) http://plato.stanford.edu/entries/hobbes-moral/.

[19] Samantha Besson, *The Morality of Conflict: Reasonable Disagreement and the Law* (Hart Publishing, 2005) 126.

[20] Celeste Friend, *Social Contract Theory*, Internet Encyclopedia of Philosophy www.iep.utm.edu/soc-cont/.

[21] Ibid.

[22] James Fieser, *Classics in Political Philosophy* (2012) ch 11.

laws and oblige enforcement of the social contract which the law constitutes. Since the authority has power to exercise absolute sovereignty especially with power and authority to mete out punishment for any breaches of the social contract, authority can be harsh and society is being obliged to comply in order to avoid the lawless State of Nature.

Hence according to Hobbes' theory, citizens are bound to obey the law and to submit all their individual rights in return for protection and security as a form of contract. Having said that, however oppressive a law may be to its citizens, it is still deemed enforceable and binding and nothing is immoral or unjust, therefore, to go against a law is in fact unjust. It can be said that justice is a notion of social contract of individuals and its state. From here it can be clearly seen that Hobbes' theory would affirm Socrates' view in which should he escape from prison he is in fact acting unjustly and any act which contradicts such enforced law is in breach of the social contract.

5.4 John Locke

John Locke, (1632–1704), an English philosopher had a different argument concerning social contract from that of his fellow country man and older contemporary Thomas Hobbes re the social contract and also political governance. According to Locke, the State of Nature is a state of complete and absolute freedom and liberty to conduct one's life however he or she pleases, being free from interference of others; still, this is not a state without morality.[23] Though the State of Nature possesses no civil authority or government to enforce punishments and penalizes transgressions of the people against the law, it is not uncivilized. The State of Nature is pre-political but not pre-moral.[24] Citizens are assumed to be equal to one another and equally capable of discovering and being bound by the Law of Nature. The Law of Nature, as per Locke, is the basis of all morality given to us by God with the commandment to not harm others with regards to one's life, liberty and possession. Since we are all made equal to God one cannot take away what is rightfully his.

Hence, under Locke's theory, the State of Nature is a state of liberty where persons are free to pursue their own interests and plans free from interference of the State. Locke however states that the State of Nature is not the same as the state of war, but it can devolve into a state of war, particularly when one declares war on another by disrupting one's liberty. Hence, in order to ensure harmonization in a society, society shall surrender some degree of its natural rights in favour of a government, which are viewed as an able protector of rights of the society. Locke is a known advocate of limited government in which his natural right theory presages that governments (or administrative regimes) hold an obligation with limited powers over their citizens

[23] Fiend (n 1).

[24] Ibid.

and can at any time, when they abuse their power, be overthrown by the citizens.[25] Ultimately his contentions shows that the State of Nature has to conform with and prioritizes one's freedom and liberty.

Since in the State of Nature there is an absence of an unfeigned civil authority, once a war begins it is more likely to be prolonged. Hence, in a similar approach to Hobbes, in a minute gage, Locke champions the notion of creating a government by consent through the establishment of a "social contract" within congenial societies based on voluntary agreement for care and protection to enforce and safeguard each citizen.[26] However, unlike Hobbes, Locke goes further by contending that government must respect the rights of the individuals by establishing limited government.[27] In the *Second Treatise of Government*, Locke asserted that men in the State of Nature are free and equal and at liberty to do as they please, but limited to the bounds of law of nature.[28] This limitation itself separates Locke's philosophical view from Hobbes.

Under Locke's theory, political society exists when men come together in the State of Nature and agree to give up the executive power to punish transgressor to the public power of a government. Having done this, individuals are then subjected to the will of the majority, in simpler words; society mutually agrees to leave the State of Nature and form one body, submitting themselves to the will of that body.[29]

However, Locke viewed that whenever executive power of a government devolves into a tyranny, by either dissolving the legislature or denying fundamental rights of individuals, the resulting tyranny is said to be putting themselves into the State of nature, and later into a state of war with the people themselves.[30] Therefore, in such a situation, the people have the right to self-defence as they had before making the compact to the establishment. This means that when protection from the government is no longer present or when tyranny emerges who act against the interest of the people, society as a whole have the right to resist the authority. Since Locke did not envision the State of Nature as rigidly as Hobbes, he can imagine situations where one would be rejecting a particular civil government and returning to the State of Nature for the betterment of the society by creating a better civil government.

If Locke's theory were to be made applicable to the situation and trial of Socrates, it is likely that Locke would have held that the escape from prison would **not** amount to an unjust act since the basis of Locke's theory of social contract is to retain one's right to freedom and liberty. This is based on the fact that Locke's theory is heavily dependent on the Law of Nature and not the laws set by the government. This Law of Nature exists to uphold the will and interest of the people as a whole hence, if government and authority acts in oppression, the people have after 'a long train

[25]Patrick J Connolly, *John Locke (1632–1704)*, Internet Encyclopedia of Philosophy http://www.iep.utm.edu/locke/.

[26]Steven Forde, *John Locke and the Natural Law and Natural Rights Tradition* (Web page, 2011) http://www.nlnrac.org/earlymodern/locke.

[27]Ibid.

[28]John Locke, *Second Treaties of Government: of Civil Government: Book 2* (1691).

[29]Fiend (n 20).

[30]Fieser (n 22) ch 14.

of Actings' have or should have the right of revolution.[31] Though admittedly it is hard to state that even Locke would have classified *ex hypothesi* Socrates' escape from prison and for that matter Aristotle's fleeing Athens – it needs to be pointed out that Aristotle, unlike Socrates had not had his day in court and had not being sentenced to any penal punishment – as an 'act of revolution'. Still, it is arguably that the social contract as espoused by Locke (different one from that of either Socrates or Hobbes) would be more kindly disposed and would arguably not rigidly oppose the hypothetical escape from prison of Socrates a course of action that Socrates had adamantly refused to take.

5.5 Jean-Jacques Rousseau

John Jacques Rousseau, 1712–1778, was a French philosopher who gave a new interpretation to the theory of social contract, as seen in his work *The Social Contract*[32] and '*Emile*'.[33] According to Rousseau, the Social Contract is not a historical fact rather it is a hypothetical construction of reasons.[34] Rousseau believes that before the existence of the Social Contract, like Locke's theory, the life and the State of Nature of society was complete and perfect and there was equality among men. People lived in solitary and uncomplicated lives with few needs which were easily satisfied by nature.[35]

However, as time goes by, humanity began to face changes particularly in the area of increment of population which causes people to segregate into smaller families and communities. Division of labour begins to take place within and between families, and discoveries and inventions arose.[36] The gruesome changes introduce competitiveness in the society which causes and lead to shame, envy, discontentment, and pride. Essentially, as per Rousseau, the invention of private property was the pivotal moment in humanity's evolution out of a simple perfect state to one which is consumed by greed, competition and vanity, hence causing inequality and vice.[37] Rousseau contended that the situation causes humanity to fall from grace out of the State of Nature.

Having introduced private property, inequality become more pronounced, social classes began to develop. Eventually, the upperclassmen, in their own interests, created a government that would protect the private property of them form those who do not possess it. The establishment of government took place through a contract which purports to promote equality and protection for the society.

[31] John Locke, *Right to Revolution, Second Treatise*. (1689) ch 3, ss 224, 225.

[32] Jean Jacques Rousseau, *The Social Contract*, G.D.H. Cole (trans) (1762).

[33] Jean Jacques Rousseau, *Emile* (1712).

[34] Fiend (n 20).

[35] Ibid.

[36] Ibid.

[37] Jean Jacques Rousseau, *Discourse on the Origin and Foundation of Inequality among Men* (1755).

In Rousseau's *The Social Contract*, he quoted that "Man was born free, and he is everywhere in chains".[38] This means that men are essentially free and were free in the State of Nature, but evolution and progress of civilization had depleted it in the expense of dependence, economics and social inequalities. However, the fundamental philosophical problem is that it is impossible for men to restore freedom and reconciling to the State of Nature by succumbing to the force and coercion of another. Hence for this purpose, Rousseau recommended that society could surrender their rights not to a single individual but to the community as a whole which he termed as a "general will", created through agreement with other free and equal persons.[39]

The Sovereign is thus formed when free and equal persons come together and agree to create a new single body directed to achieve the catering of good of all. Hence just as individual will directed towards individual interests, general will is directed to the common good and understood and agreed collectively. Given this, individuals cannot be given the liberty to decide whether it is in their own interest to fulfil their duty to the sovereign. They must be made to conform to the general will.[40] This implies an extremely strong and direct form of democracy.

Therefore, in determining what ought to be good and just in the Social Contract is dependent in the resolution of the collective individual. If it is collectively agreed that certain actions do not conform to the general will such acts would be deemed unjust and unlawful. Similarly if it is collectively agreed that an act is just it should be upheld and any act violating or restricting such act would be deemed oppressive and unjust. Hence, Rousseau could arguably state that in Socrates' situation, whether or not such escape would be justified lies in the hand of "those who understand justice" as contended by Socrates in the *Crito*, Since the concept of general will is dependent on the opinion and decision of the collective of the community and since the guilt of Socrates was determined by a majority of only 30 votes albeit the sentence of death meted out to Socrates was given by (360–140 = 120 vote majority of the jurors) we find it difficult to state unequivocally whether that majority in a jury trial of Athens would have been considered to reflect Rousseau's 'general will' or not.

5.6 Herbert Lionel Adolphus Hart

H. L. A. Hart, (1907–1992) in the notable Hart and Fuller debate on the fidelity of the law stated that the ideal of fidelity to law may be better understood primarily on the consideration that "law as it is" and "law as it ought to be" must first be clearly distinguished following the concept of legal positivism.[41] Therefore, according to

---

[38] Rousseau (n 32).

[39] Fiend (n 20).

[40] Ibid.

[41] Stephen Hlawatsch, 'Separation of Law and Morals? A Debate about Legal Validity and its Implications for Moral Criticism' (2010) https://mafiadoc.com/separation-of-law-and-morals-unet-universitt-wien_5a22f95c1723ddd337ecc6d8.html.

Hart, legal validity is to be determined based on rule of recognition and the condition that it is appropriately legislated by the Legislature or the regime in power and obtain legal status.[42] Hence, morality is not the only essential criterion in ascertaining validity of law.[43]

Following Hart's approach, taking into consideration the Nazi laws, the laws of the Nazi regime, even though it deviated from morality, is in fact legally valid. The implemented law was legislated by the ruling regime, though argued to be oppressive, people living under that regime abided by their law fearing that their lives and security would be jeopardised if they do not adhere to them. Such obedience would tantamount to acceptance and thereby fulfilled the requirements of the rule of recognition regardless of the fact that the laws enacted were oppressive in disposition.[44] Therefore, Hart firmly was of the view the Nazi era legal system was a valid legal system.[45]

It is to be noted that Hart did not totally disregard the relevance of morality. He would agree that where social regulation is paramount, law and morality may overlap and co-exist.[46] Therefore the when an enacted law is deemed immoral there is no need for the subjects to blindly obey the law. Though the subjects living under that law have the legal obligation to adhere by the law, it however, did not take away their rights to reject that law on moral considerations and vent their criticism.[47] By Hart's definition, if a law passed to be oppressive it may be concluded to be questionable nevertheless it is still deemed to be valid and enforceable.

Hart's approach is solely on what is law ought to be valid law regardless or morality, Hence, in Socrates' situation, Hart would view such escape, under the rule of recognition, to be in non-conformity with it as it believed that law is deemed to be the law hence it should be abide by the citizens however oppressive or immoral it may be.

5.7 Lon Luvois Fuller

According to Lon Fuller, (1902–1978) law is not a neutral concept but rather that law exemplifies inner morality. "Inner morality of law" relates fundamentally to the law making procedure whereby the lawmaker decides which rule of substantive law is to

[42]HLA Hart, 'Positivism and the Separation of Law and Morals' (1958) 71(4) *Harvard Law Review* 593–629, 603.

[43]HLA Hart, *The Concept of Law* (Clarendon Law Series, 2nd ed, 1994) 181.

[44]Ibid. 100.

[45]Jeremy Waldron, 'Positivism and Legality: Hart's Equivocal Response to Fuller' (2008) 83 *New York University Law Review* 1135, 1139.

[46]Hart (1958) (n 42) 622–623.

[47]Hart (1994) (n 43) 199.

be applied in a specific case.[48] Fuller is of the view that it is impossible to separate law from morals. This means that if a law is immoral, it is invalid law and therefore *void ab initio*.

Fuller opined that it is not sufficient for legal validity to depend on the acceptance of Hart's rule of recognition. The definitive rule for legality is the rule of recognition but the same is to be said for morality.[49] To Fuller, the nature of the laws made valid by the rule of recognition must be considered. These 'laws' are accepted generally by the people because they perceive them as right and necessary, as something good and promoting good order. This then, showed a 'merger' between law and morality as opposed to Hart's 'intersection' of the two.[50]

Fuller's approach also advocates for the legal system to have specific characteristics i.e. morals that command the fidelity to law. As said by Fuller, the integrity of the law is dependent on morality and it is "morality that makes law possible".[51] He proposed that eight requirements must be satisfied to be valid law as follows:

1. There must be general rules formed to steer certain acts;
2. The public or at least the people addressed by the rules, must know these rules;
3. The rules should be prospective rather than retrospective in nature;
4. Rules should be certain (unambiguous) and understandable;
5. They should not be conflicting with one another;
6. They should not demand the impossible;
7. The rules should be relatively established; and
8. There should be consistency between the announced rules and the administration and implementation of those rules.[52]

Fuller described the eight conditions as "procedural version of natural law" and the ones that meet all these requirements will typically be a sound and just legal system.[53] Fuller asserts that morality and law come hand in hand in which in the absence of the other the law becomes invalid.

Therefore, for the act of Socrates to be deemed as unjust, the law must first be a valid law as what is prescribed by Fuller. Fuller believes that when a law contains no morality it shall be deemed unlawful hence, is not valid. Since Fuller would have deemed the laws and indeed the acts of the Jury in sentencing Socrates to death was unjust Fuller might well have considered that it would **not** have been unjust for Socrates to have escaped from prison. We are of the view that Socrates' notion of

[48]Edwin W Tucker, 'The Morality of Law, by Lon L. Fuller' (1965) 40 *Indiana Law Journal* 270, 271.

[49]Stephan Hlawatsch, 'Separation of Law and Morals? A Debate about Legal Validity and Its Implications for Moral Criticism' (2010) University of Vienna, Institute for Philosophy, Legality and Legitimacy https://mafiadoc.com/separation-of-law-and-morals-unet-universitt-wien_5a22f95c1723ddd337ecc6d8.html.

[50]Lon L Fuller, 'Positivism and Fidelity to Law – A Reply to Professor Hart' (1958) 71 *Harvard Law Review* 630, 639.

[51]Ibid. 644–646.

[52]Lon L Fuller, *The Morality of Law* (Yale University Press, 1964) 39.

[53]Ibid. 97.

absolute obligation to obey even unjust laws or unjust sentences does not conform to Fuller's notion as indicate in his famous debate with H. L. A. Hart. Fuller subscribes to the view that unjust laws are no laws at all or 'perversions of laws'.

5.8 Conclusion

The philosophers and jurists' views and what we think would be their views on Socrates' refusal to escape from prison is necessarily subjective and among them the 'oldest' philosopher so to speak to (indirectly) comment on Socrates' refusal to escape from prison as discussed in this chapter is Aristotle. Aristotle was born 78 years after Socrates died and Aristotle apparently did not specifically comment on the 'social contract' and 'repaying injustice with injustice' stated in the *Crito*.

The latter philosophers of what can be called the 'Enlightenment philosophers' Hobbes, Locke and Rousseau did have their own social contract theories and we have tried to apply them the reasons given by Plato in the *Crito*. Compared to the earlier philosophers, H. L. A. Hart and Lon Fuller can be considered as contemporary jurists. Though they may or may not have published their views on Plato's *Crito* we have attempted to apply their views on what can be considered the greatest 'non-escape' from prison story in the history of Western philosophy.

Bibliography

Books

Besson, Samantha, *The Morality of Conflict: Reasonable Disagreement and the Law* (Hart Publishing, 2005)
Fearn, Nicholas, *Zeno and the Tortoise* (Atlantic Books, 2001)
Fuller, Lon L, *The Morality of Law* (Yale University Press, 1964)
Hart, HLA, *The Concept of Law* (Clarendon Law Series, 2nd ed, 1994)
Hobbes, Thomas, *The Leviathan* (1651)
Huppes-Cluysenaer, Liesbeth and Nuno MMS Coelho (eds), *Aristotle and the Philosophy of Law: Theory, Practice and Justice* (Springer, 2013)
Locke, John, *Right to Revolution, Second Treatise* (1689)
Locke, John, *Second Treaties of Government: of Civil Government: Book 2* (1691)
Philips, David D, *The Law of Ancient Athens* (University of Michigan Press, 2013)
Plato, *Crito*, translated by Benjamin Jowett (C. Scribner's Sons, 1871)
Rousseau, Jean Jacques, *Emile* (1712)
Rousseau, Jean Jacques, *Discourse on the Origin and Foundation of Inequality among Men* (1755)
Rousseau, Jean Jacques, *The Social Contract*, G.D.H. Cole (trans) (1762)
Strauss, Leo, *Persecution and the Art of Writing* (University of Chicago Press, 2013)
The Concise Columbia Encyclopedia, 'Plato: Founder of the Academy' (Columbia University Press, 1991)

Articles

Fuller, Lon L, 'Positivism and Fidelity to Law – A Reply to Professor Hart' (1958) 71 *Harvard Law Review* 630

Hart, HLA, 'Positivism and the Separation of Law and Morals' (1958) 71(4) *Harvard Law Review* 593

Hlawatsch, Stephan, 'Separation of Law and Morals? A Debate about Legal Validity and Its Implications for Moral Criticism' (2010) University of Vienna, Institute for Philosophy, Legality and Legitimacy https://mafiadoc.com/separation-of-law-and-morals-unet-universitt-wien_5a22f95c1723ddd337ecc6d8.html

Tucker, Edwin W, 'The Morality of Law, by Lon L. Fuller' (1965) 40 *Indiana Law Journal* 270

Waldron, Jeremy, 'Positivism and Legality: Hart's Equivocal Response to Fuller' (2008) 83 *New York University Law Review* 1135

Other

Biography.com, *Aristotle* (Web page, 2015) http://www.biography.com/people/aristotle-9188415

Biography.com, *Plato*, (Web page, 2015) http://www.biography.com/people/plato-9442588

Connolly, Patrick J, *John Locke (1632–1704)*, Internet Encyclopedia of Philosophy http://www.iep.utm.edu/locke/

Fieser, James, *Classics in Political Philosophy* (2012) https://www.utm.edu/staff/jfieser/class/410-pol/classics-in-pol-phil.htm

Forde, Steven, *John Locke and the Natural Law and Natural Rights Tradition* (Web page, 2011) http://www.nlnrac.org/earlymodern/locke

Friend, Celeste, *Social Contract Theory*, Internet Encyclopedia of Philosophy www.iep.utm.edu/soc-cont/

Stanford Encyclopedia of Philosophy, *Aristotle's Political Theory* (1998) http://plato.stanford.edu/entries/aristotle-politics/

Stanford Encyclopedia of Philosophy, *Hobbes's Moral and Political Philosophy* (Web page, 2002) http://plato.stanford.edu/entries/hobbes-moral/

University of Missouri-Kansas City School of Law, *Criminal Procedure in Ancient Greece and the Trial of Socrates* http://law2.umkc.edu/faculty/projects/ftrials/socrates/greekcrimpro.html

Chapter 6
What Would Socrates Have Said on Two Conversations About Harbouring Runway Slaves and Running Away from Slavery in *Uncle Tom's Cabin* by Harriet Beecher Stowe

Chew Yi Ting, Kan Da Xing, and Myint Zan

Abstract There is no direct and concrete evidence that Socrates opposed = the slavery system as practised in fourth century Before the Current Era (BCE) in Athens. Let's assume that Socrates had endorsed the system of slavery practised in his lifetime in Athens of over 2400 years ago. Would he still have done so if he were to 'come back' to the nineteenth century America? Looking in the light of the movement in mid-nineteenth century America to abolish slavery, if Socrates isn't persuaded that the slavery system should be abolished, it must be because he holds strictly to his views when he is (or was) still the Socrates of 470-399 BCE. We analyse Socrates' arguments and apply them to the situation of the slavery system practised in the mid-nineteenth century America, to discern what Socrates' view would be in this context. Would the great philosopher still choose to endorse the slavery system? Will his arguments stand up against an outspoken thoughts of a slave in the mid-nineteenth century? In this Chapter we postulate what Socrates might have said on two conversations regarding harbouring runway slaves in contrary to the existing laws then and the act of George Harris' running away from the bondage of slavery again breaching the existing laws as depicted in Harriet Beecher Stowe's *Uncle Tom's Cabin* published in mid-nineteenth century in the United States. Our analysis of what Socrates might have stated is primarily based on Socrates' arguments (as narrated by Plato) in the *Crito*. This article presents Socrates' arguments and attitude towards slavery by linking, delinking, contextualising and decontextualizing as the case may be certain aspects of two classical texts written 2400 years apart: Plato's *Crito* and Harriet Beecher Stowe's *Uncle Tom's Cabin*.

Keywords and Concepts *Crito* by Plato · Socrates' attitudes towards slavery · *Uncle Tom's cabin* by Harriet Beecher Stowe · Senator and Mrs. Bird conversation in *Uncle Tom's cabin* and what would socrates have said about it · George and Mr. Harris' conversation in *Uncle Tom's cabin* and what would socrates have said about it

---

Chew Yi Ting, LL.B, yiting1992@gmail.com, Kan Da Xing, LL.B, vennie.co@gmail.com and Myint Zan, myintzan@yahoo.com.au.

M. Zan (ed.), *Legal Education and Legal Traditions: Selected Essays*,
SpringerBriefs in Environment, Security, Development and Peace,
https://doi.org/10.1007/978-3-030-50903-3_6

6.1 Introduction

6.1.1 Socrates'Attitude About Slavery During 430 BCE

An analysis on Socrates view on slavery can be discerned from the writings of Plato, *Socrates' Dialogue withMeno, a slave*. In the *Meno* in the dialogue with Meno's slave, the slave managed to give answers even though the answers given might not have been correct. Socrates was patient enough to correct and teach the slave. However, the dialogue in *Meno* only shows that Socrates thinks it is the right of slaves to speak just as others, but that alone does not indicate that Socrates condemned the slavery system.

In another dialogue, *Gorgias*, Plato was of view that it was right for the 'better' to rule over the 'inferior':

> ...nature herself intimates that it is just for the better to have more than the worse, the more powerful than the weaker; and in many ways she shows, among men as well as among animals, and indeed among whole cities and races, that justice consists in the superior ruling over and having more than the inferior.[1]

6.2 Socrates' View on Slavery in the Mid-Nineteenth Century

If Socrates were to be brought back to life in the nineteenth century America, in the 1850s, would he change his mind about slavery? No longer in the ancient Greek society, the situation may be somewhat different if Socrates were to be 'transported' to the mid-nineteenth century.

We are of the view that the issue of slavery during the time of Socrates (470-399 BCE) was not as 'bad' as in the mid-nineteenth century. In Athens 2400 years ago there might have been selling of women and children into slavery but this did not cause as much problem to the people in Athens as it did it mid-nineteenth century America.

The issue of slavery became increasingly serious when internal slave trade became the major economic activity in the United States in the year 1815.[2] Despite the fact that slaves were hardly given any rights, slaves were beneficial to the State in the economic sense. In other words, slaves were used to develop the State.[3] Even though Socrates agreed that the 'better should rule over the "inferior"', he did not go so far as saying the better could trade the inferior as goods!

---

[1]Plato, *Gorgias*, 447a–453a.

[2]Steven Deyle, 'The Irony of Liberty: Origins of the Domestic Slave Trade' 12(1) (Spring 1992) *Journal of the Early Republic* pp. 37–62.

[3]Jim Pearson and John Robertson, *Slavery in the Nineteenth Century* (University of California Press, 1999) 5.

In the early nineteenth century in the United States slavery was a central institution and was accepted as normal by many. However, this broad acceptance of slavery began to be challenged in the Revolutionary Era. Such challenges came from several sources, partly form Revolutionary ideals, partly from a new evangelical religious commitment that stressed the equality of all Christians.[4]

One might observe that *Uncle Tom's Cabin* focuses on illustrating the effect of slavery on families perhaps arousing strong sentiments among some or most readers to empathize with the plight of the slaves. *Uncle Tom's Cabin* is known as anti-slavery novel.[5] It illustrates a shift in the mind-set of the society, from thinking slavery is normal and slaves are necessary, to focusing on the rights of slaves as humans and perhaps later with the *Emancipation Proclamation* of President Abraham Lincoln –at least on paper equal rights as other citizens of the United States.

As increasing number of people advocated for the abolition of slavery and slavery in the United States came to an end in the late nineteenth century. This shows that enacted laws and the 'sense of right and wrong' are variable depending on the social atmosphere of that particular period of time. This is why slavery was once permitted and justified by the law but later became universally accepted as illegal.

If we put Socrates in the mid-nineteenth century, there is a good chance that Socrates' thoughts about slavery could be affected we hope and 'informed' Socrates so that he would adjust his views. Public opinion, nature of society, and surrounding environment has begun to be changed in mid-nineteenth century America. In mid-nineteenth century United States the necessity, indeed the morality and legality of slavery has been publicly challenged.

In the fourth century Before the Current Era even if he had not endorsed slavery Socrates had not specifically critiqued it. Although known as a non-conformist would Socrates 'conform' to or reject the emergent anti-slavery sentiments among at least the abolitionists at that time in mid-nineteenth century America? The efforts to abolish slavery in the United States eventually changed the views of most members of society. If Socrates were to come back to the nineteenth century America would he have been swayed by the movement against slavery or not?

6.3 Socrates' View on Conversation 1

6.3.1 Introduction

In this conversation, between Senator Bird from the state of Ohio and his wife in *Uncle Tom's Cabin* Mrs Bird argued that a law which forbids people from helping

[4]Independence Hall Association in Philadelphia, *Revolutionary Changes and Limitations: Slavery*. http://www.ushistory.org/us/13d.asp.

[5]Harriet Beecher Stowe Center, *Impact of Uncle Tom's Cabin, Slavery, and the Civil War*. https://www.kyrene.org/cms/lib/AZ01001083/Centricity/Domain/3828/Impact%20of%20Uncle%20Toms%20Cabin.docx.

'poor coloured folks'[6] shouldnot have been passed or in effect the 'existing law' which prohibits the harbouring of run-away slaves can be ignored. On the other hand, Senator Bird was of the opinion that his wife should not put her personal feelings while giving her views on the *Anti-Fugitive Act*—which the Senator had helped draft—which prohibited the harbouring of run-away slaves. The Senator, in effect, stated that in view of the great public interests involved personal feelings regarding the slavery issue should be set aside.[7]

6.3.2 Analysis of Relevant Arguments from Socrates' Viewpoint

6.3.2.1 Religious Argument

Arguments made by Mary Bird (the wife of the Senator) based on Christianity and those of Socrates were from different points of view. This would be so, in large part, because during the time of Socrates Christianity did not exist.

Mary Bird's arguments were premised on her belief of the (moral) duty of a State to enact laws which conforms to what Mary considered to be Christian values (i.e., to help the poor and needy). Socrates's arguments made over 2200 years earlier were basically about the obligation to obey the law passed by the state on various grounds to be discussed below.

According to Mary, the Bible should prevail over the law of the state. Besides, God will never bring on public evils. Therefore, she strongly believed that God wants people to do good to the society. Thus, it is clear that Mary did not agree with the new law that was enacted by the Ohio Legislature that prohibited any one from aiding run-away slaves from Kentucky or other states in the ante-bellum South.

In this regard it can be stated that Socrates was apparently not a religious sceptic (notwithstanding his 'maverick' reputation). There is no record of his having been particularly scornful of religion.[8] On this point, Socrates would most probably agree with Mary that the State should see to it that there is no law which bring public evils.

Mary viewed that turning away a poor, shivering and hungry creature from the door simply because he was a run-away was unchristian and it was against the religious teaching.[9] Based on the fact that Socrates believe in God, (albeit historically, chronologically it could not have been the Christian God[10]) it is reasonable to assume that Socrates would agree with Mary not to do any unchristian activity. Socrates seems to be willing to sacrifice a great extent for his religious belief, as he said: 'I do not

[6]In the mid-nineteenth century almost all of the slaves were 'Blacks' ('coloured').

[7]Harriet Beecher Stowe, *Uncle Tom's Cabin* (John P Jewett & Co, 1852) 120.

[8]James Rachels and Stuart Rachels (eds), *The Legacy of Socrates: Essays in Moral Philosophy* (Columbia University Press, 2007).

[9]Stowe (n 6) 119.

[10]Plato, *Apology* (Hackett Publishing Company, 2000).

have the leisure to engage in public affairs to any extent, nor indeed to look after my own, but I live in great poverty because of my service to the god.'[11]

However, this is subject to the assumption that Socrates' religious belief in God is similar with the Christian teachings as believed by Mary which, according to her, encompass the precept that one should not turn away poor persons merely because they were slaves.

6.3.2.2 Paternalistic Argument

However, we submit that Socrates most probably would not have agreed with Mary's suggestion and eventual action to harbour the run-away slave Eliza in *Uncle Tom's Cabin.* In the *Crito,* Socrates said to the friend Crito that he had heard 'the Laws' saying:

> … since you have been born and brought up and educated, can you deny, in the first place, that you were our child and slave…And if it [your country] leads you out to war, to be wounded or killed, you must comply, and *it is just that this should be so* – you must not give way or retreat or abandon your position. Both in war and in the law courts and everywhere else *you must do whatever your city and your country commands, or else persuade it that justice is on your side…*[12]

Applying this paternalistic argument, Socrates most probably would not have agreed with Mrs Mary Bird. Socrates would say that Mary Bird has a right to leave the country (or the State of Ohio) if she was unsatisfied with the laws of Ohio, in order to avoid obeying the *Anti-Fugitive Act*. However, if she did not do that she has an obligation to either obey the law passed by the government or persuade the State to amend the law. Since she has not done these Socrates could probably argue that Mary should not harbour a run-away slave contrary to the existing laws.

6.3.2.3 Gratitude Argument

If Socrates were in mid-nineteenth century America and privy as above to the conversations between Senator Bird and his wife, Socrates would have argued that the laws of Ohio would have said that the Senator should obey them as they have provided him, education etc. and even the Senator's high position in the society is due to these 'laws'. Our submission extrapolates—later to be elaborated and qualified—what *The Laws* said to Socrates (and which Socrates in turn said the 'sound of what the Laws said resonated in his ears and he could not hear anything else' as stated in the *Crito*) to the debate between Senator Bird and his wife in *Uncle Tom's Cabin.* The issues discussed would be whether the Birds should harbour in their house albeit only for a night the escaped slave Eliza.

---

[11] Ibid 23.

[12] Plato, *The Last Days of Socrates*: *Crito-Justice and Duty (ii)* (Penguin Classics, 2003) 91.

Socrates's could have said to Mary Bird that Mary's comments indicated she was not a good 'citizen' to the state who has nurtured her like a parent since she was born. Both Senator and Mary had a social contract with the state and they must be grateful with what the state gave them. They should not break the law even if the law is unjust to the slaves.

6.3.2.4 Social Contract Argument

We find that Socrates would most probably agree with Senator Bird in (at least initially in his conversation with his wife) opting to obey the law which prohibited the citizens from aiding those run-away slaves from Kentucky and would choose not to harbour them as it clearly violates the country's law.

Applying the social contract argument, Senator Bird who had chosen to stay in his country would have an obligation to obey the law since he did not choose to leave his country when he attained the age of majority. He is deemed to have accepted the social contract and therefore had an obligation to obey the law. Due to this, we find that Socrates would support Senator Bird's statement as to not harbour run-away slaves and continue to abide by the institution and practice of slavery as they should be bound by the existing laws of Ohio as Socrates was also bound by the Athenian laws not to escape from prison.

6.3.2.5 Socrates' Possible View

We believe that Socrates would most probably not agree with the act of harbouring the run-away slaves (eventually) by Senator Bird and his wife Mary. Generally, Socrates' point of view is that one can choose to leave the state if one does not like the law of the particular state. However, if one chooses to stay in the state this would create a presumption that the concerned person agrees to obey all the laws in the State and accept the social rules notwithstanding whether they are good or bad, just or unjust laws and rules.

The Senator who has voted for the Ohio law has obligation to Ohio and to obey its laws regarding escaped slaves.

Ultimately, we believe Socrates would say something like this:

> Dear Senator and Mrs Bird I would refrain myself from saying much against the Laws or the State of Ohio, for I am an Athenian, and I do not live here. I have no right to destroy such Laws and all the more so you too also had no such right. You have lived in the state of Ohio for such a long time and your state nurtured both of you. Senator and Mrs Bird, if you feel deep pity for the escaped slaves and the laws which prohibited them from being given safe harbour you must try to amend or abolish those laws instead of breaking the law which you yourself has voted to support it.

6.4 Socrates' View on Conversation 2

6.4.1 Introduction

In this conversation, we need to analyse why George tried to escape from his Master before we consider what Socrates' might have said to the conversations between George and Mr Wilson: George being the slave, contrary to existing laws at that time was running away from his Master. During his childhood, his mother and sister were taken away from him and both of them were sold as slaves. George was left alone, without his family to love him.[13]

6.4.2 Extrapolating a Few Arguments from the Crito *and Applying to George's Situation in* Uncle Tom's Cabin

6.4.2.1 Experts' Opinion Argument

In the *Crito* Socrates argued that in deciding one's action(s) one should not listen to the 'opinion of the many' but only to those of the experts.Socrates made this statement to respond to and 'solace' Crito's concern and anxiety that he (Crito) will be blamed if the public (the many) came to learn that he (Crito) did not help Socrates to escape from prison notwithstanding that he had had the chance and the monetary resources to effect Socrates' escape. We are of the view that applying Socrates exhortation to heed only to the opinion of the experts might not arguably assist Socrates in weighing his attitude towards George's escape which was close to completion when the conversation between George and Mr Wilson took place. Arguably, in the Southern state of Kentucky the public opinion would be against George's fleeing from his slave Master. Most of the public opinion in George's time and place (mid-nineteenth century Kentucky) would have disapproved of George's action of running away. We further submit that George did not heed (at all) the opinion of the many slave-owners and non-slaves who are not slave owners as well. Additionally perhaps this can be 'stretched' to argue that in this context that Socrates –just- might consider that George should not 'heed' the 'opinion of the many' or the public. If George were to be caught during his escape the 'many' in the slave-owning State of Kentucky would have approved of '//[George] [being] abuse[d] and half kill[ed] and s[old] … down the river'.[14]

If George can be said not to listen to the 'public opinion' did he listen to the experts as Socrates has exhorted his friend Crito in the *Crito*? Who then would be

---

[13] Harriet Beecher Stowe, *Uncle Tom's Cabin (1852), Chapter XI (In Which Property Gets into an Improper State of Mind)*. http://manybooks.net/titles/stowehar203203.html.
[14] Stowe (n 6) 164.

'the experts'? The sage-philosopher Socrates would have been the expert. We submit that the expert Socrates, initially at least, would not have approved or endorsed the act of George Harris running away from the bondage of slaver merely based on the fact because running away from slavery was contrary to the public opinion in Kentucky.

As stated in earlier sections the presumption is that Socrates approved of the institution and practice of slavery 2400 years ago. What matters is whether the expert(s) (apart from Socrates himself) would have agreed to such an act not in Socrates own case but in the case of George. It is unclear in the *Crito* who exactly is the expert, but what is clear is that Socrates espoused that public opinion did not and should not affect the (il)legality nor the (im)morality of running away from prison of Socrates himself. But here in George's situation his partly completed and intention to complete his escape from slavery—Socrates *is*(was) the expert and what would he have said to that? Other arguments discernible from the *Crito* would be considered before we submit what, in our opinion, could have been Socrates' views and suggestions to George the would-be and eventual escapee from slavery.

6.4.2.2 Gratitude Argument

Form the viewpoint of the gratitude argument in the *Crito*, Socrates refused to run away from prison because he had (in so few words) owed so much to Athens. Socrates was unable to bring himself to run away from prison because he had heard the Laws scolding him:

> ... Have you had anything against the Laws which deal with children's upbringing and education, *such as you had yourself*? Are you not grateful to those of us Laws which were put in control of this, *for requiring your father to give you an education in music and gymnastics*? (emphasis added)[15]

Therefore, it can be seen that the gratitude argument only applies to Socrates or perhaps persons in similar situations as him such as Senator and Mrs Bird who actually have received the benefit of upbringing and education. Socrates would have no discernible reason to complain of the treatment Athens had accorded him a least till his arrest and trial. We submit that the learned philosopher should readily see that especially the 'gratitude' argument would not apply to the 'case' of George, the harsh treatment indeed the enslavement that George Harris suffered at the hands of his (soon to be as the conversation in *Uncle Tom's Cabin* proceeds) of his former Master under the imprimatur of the then existing laws of Kentucky. Indeed George's Master put up an advertisement that 'will give four hundred dollars... for satisfactory proof that he [George] has been killed'.[16] Wasn't that sufficient proof of how badly his Master has treated George? As George exclaimed in his conversation with Mr Wilson '... what country have I, or any one like me, born of slave mothers? What laws are there for us?' This searing query from the escapee slave George compellingly

[15]Plato (n 11).

[16]Stowe (n 6) 157.

indicates that he was not born or brought up as a beneficiary of his State—very much *unlike* Socrates. Kentucky Laws did not give rights to a proper upbringing or education that deserves any gratitude in return from George.

6.4.2.3 Social Contract Argument

The social contract argument also does not apply to George because there was no social contract between George Harris and Kentucky in the first place. In the *Crito* the social contract is that Socrates will obey the State in gratitude to the education and upbringing of The Laws have provided to Socrates.[17] However, what Kentucky did was, in the words of George Harris, 'to crush us [slaves], and keep us down'.[18]Therefore, Socrates would or at least—should—probably conclude that there is no social contract between Kentucky and George, because there were no terms regarding protection towards George in Kentucky's constitution, or 'social contract'. Indeed the law of Kentucky provided the imprimatur for his Master(s) to enslave George.

Further, Socrates mentioned that he entered into the agreement willingly with Athens when he decided to stay in Athens despite having the opportunity to leave Athens. The Laws of Athens gave Socrates the choice to leave Athens with all his properties if he is not satisfied with them.[19] In the case of George Harris, he did not voluntarily enter into any contract with Kentucky, nor did he choose to stay in the state. This can be seen from the fact that he was running away from Kentucky to Ohio. Also, George Harris did explain to Mr Wilson that as slaves of Kentucky, 'We [the slaves] don't make them [Kentucky laws]—we *don't consent* to them—we have nothing to do with them' (emphasis added). Socrates would—or should—surely understand that George Harris has a better right of running away from his (so called) 'own country' than Socrates himself.

6.4.2.4 Repaying Injustice with Injustice Argument

At this stage, it is clear that the arguments discussed above are only applicable to Socrates' absolute deference if not obedience to Athenian laws but certainly were not applicable to George Harris' situation with regards to those of Kentucky. The main reason is that Socrates was well-treated as a citizen of Athens but George Harris was poorly treated and he was not (quite) a citizen of the United States. However, the principle of Socrates that 'it is never right to commit injustice or return injustice or defend one's self against injury by retaliation' which he held for a long time and

[17]Plato (n 1).

[18]Stowe (n 6) 164.

[19]Plato (n 12).

still holds before his death,[20] might be a reason Socrates might if not disagree then probably equivocate about the 'justice' of running away of George Harris.

According to Socrates, escaping from prison is an injury to the State and the Laws. This is a form of injustice because Socrates also said that 'there is no difference between injuring people and doing them an injustice'.[21] Since injustice cannot be done no matter the circumstances, Socrates firmly believed and told Crito that he would *not* escape from prison. Arguably carrying Socrates' argument *reductio ad absurdum*, the running away of George Harris' from his Master can be construed to be an 'injury' to his Master. Since it is an injury, it (arguably) becomes a form of injustice. Injustice cannot be committed even for self-defence or retaliation stated Socrates. Therefore from the perspective such a 'Socratic argument' then George Harris should have not fled from his Master.

However, a closer or indulgent analysis of the reasoning of Socrates it can be discerned or derived that the consequence of injustice done to the Laws of Athens is ultimately that the denizen(s) of Hades[22]will not welcome Socrates. As stated earlier, Socrates was not a religious sceptic: not only did he believe in his immortal soul and the after-life he apparently believe in 'Hades'. The possible injury that Socrates would deem to have been done by George is the injury to his Master/owner. The consequence of such injury is far less, because it would not anger the Laws of Hades but perhaps mainly his Master. It is likely though that his Master's 'anger' would be shared but to a lesser extent by the 'many' in the state of Kentucky. Further, a slave who runs away from his Master does not nullify the Laws of Kentucky, although it certainly was a criminal offence under the then existing law(s). It could not injure the Laws (in *The Crito* of Plato) because unlike escaping from prison, it did not deal with negating the effect of any sanctions confirmed by courts. In this regard we submit that Socrates was under a sentence of death by a Court and was in prison after such a sentence but George although his enslavement had the imprimatur of Kentucky law was not under a sentence as such by a Kentucky Court at the time of his escape.

6.4.3 Socrates' Possible View on the Fleeing (Soon to Be) Former Slave George

Based on the above, Socrates most probably would not have condemned or scolded George's fleeing away from his Master as the 'Laws' had condemned the option of escape proffered to Socrates by his friend in the *Crito*; this is because Socrates would have discerned a great difference between the treatments that George received from Kentucky compared to those which Socrates received from Athens 2300 years prior to the events depicted in Harriet Beecher Stowe's novel foregrounded in mid-nineteenth century the ante-bellum South.

[20]Ibid 89.

[21]Ibid 88.

[22]In Greek mythology god of the Underworld.

All arguments in *Crito* seem to be inapplicable except for the argument that pertains to injustice done towards another, which also becomes weaker since it is an injury towards an individual (George's Master) and not towards a State.

In order to reinforce our previous point, Philip Soper explained that: 'Socrates, after all, is under sentence of death because he refuses at his trial to cease his philosophizing-refuses, that is, to obey the law. Now, however, he accedes to the judgment and accepts the legal consequences of that refusal. So interpreted, *the Crito is not about the duty to obey at all, but about the duty to accept the legal consequences of civil disobedience*'[23](emphasis added).

Therefore, despite his view that the State and its laws should be obeyed in an almost absolute manner in a very strict sense, Socrates willingly accepted the consequences of disobedience. It is just that one should accept the legal consequences of such disobedience. Socrates would probably remind George Harris that if (in case) he is caught for disobeying the laws, he might have to accept the legal consequence of his civil disobedience, but (as discussed earlier) George's duty to accept the sentence is (we submit) far less than Socrates' duty.

In conclusion, we believe Socrates would not say anything to discourage George Harris. He might even nod in agreement when George declares proudly by saying 'I'm ready for 'em! Down south I never will go. No! if it comes to that, I can earn myself at least six feet of free soil—the first and last I shall ever own in Kentucky!',[24] which resembles Socrates' character of bravery to disobey the Athens' law by his insistence before and during his trial in 'corrupting' the minds of the young Athenians.

However, he would probably also refrain from encouraging George Harris to run away. This is based on two reasons discernible in the *Crito*. First, quoting *The Laws* Socrates quoted (apparently with approval) that 'all good patriots will eye you [Socrates] with suspicion as a destroyer of laws'.[25] Secondly, it would arguably not be in conformity with the decision of Socrates approving the institution and practice of slavery albeit as pointed earlier the nature, function and operations of slavery practised in Athens of fourth century Before the Current Era and—2300 years later—in mid-nineteenth century southern states of the United States is quite different. But, it is very likely for Socrates to change his mind about slavery when George says: 'look at me, now. Don't I sit before you, every way, just as much a man as you are? Look at my face,—look at my hands,—look at my body,' and when George drew himself up proudly; 'why am I not a man, as much as anybody?'[26]After all Socrates' arguments could further downgrade George's already degraded life of slavery if applied. There is no reason why Socrates would still hold that slaves like George are merely property, and they should not enjoy basic human rights.

---

[23]Philip Soper, 'Another Look at the *Crito*' (1996) 41 *American Journal of Jurisprudence* 103, 109.

[24]Stowe (n 6) 164.

[25]Plato (n 11) 94.

[26]Stowe (n 6) 165.

Socrates once said: 'Do you think he who rules is still a slave?... It doesn't seem likely, my good man'.[27] Ultimately, we believe Socrates would say something like this:

> Dear George, I would refrain myself from saying much against the Laws or the State of Kentucky, for I am an Athenian, and I do not live nor am I brought up here, so I have no right to destroy such Laws that are made by the Kentucky Legislature. But as I observe, George, you do not look like a slave to me, and even if you were, I no longer see you as one, for you are now ruled by no one but yourself, both physically and mentally.

6.5 Conclusion

Socrates would probably have refused to endorse slavery as it is practised in the mid-nineteenth century. Socrates, apparently the philosopher of principle could have seen the injustices and the inhumanity of the slavery system practised in some parts of the United States of America in the mid-nineteenth century.

Socrates is (using the historic present tense) a man of principle. He acts in conformity with what he thinks is right, but will accept punishment of his civil disobedience instead of running away, even if he has the option to do so as indeed he had. Arguably, Socrates might, especially in the context of the conversation between Mr Wilson and George Harris, have an opinion that slaves can escape from their enslavement as long as they accept the consequences of their own actions (should they be captured).

In *Uncle Tom's Cabin*, the Senator and his wife are persons from the upper-class of their society. As argued in the First part Socrates might suggest that since they chose to live in Ohio, they must follow its laws. Socrates might not have approved of their actions of Senator and his wife not adhering the dictates of the slavery system in Kentucky this would have been so since Socrates would deem that the Senator and wife were the beneficiaries of the State. However, if Senator and his wife truly believed that the slavery system practice in Ohio is unjust then according to Socrates they could propose to change the law. After all, wouldn't it be fair to say that the Senator has the ability to vote against the law to prohibit harbouring of slaves?

On the other hand, George is willing to fight for his personal freedom. With regards to this, Socrates might have agreed with George's right to 'be free from slavery'. Based on Socrates' own argument, by defying the law, one is trying to destroy the society, but if one does not agree with the law, he has an option to leave the state and begin a new life in the new state.[28] Hence if Socrates were to ponder or reflect on George's plight and flight (so to speak) he just might, we submit, not be critical of George's flight.

Socrates could have 'factored' in, the obvious fact the then laws in force did not allow George to 'leave the state' lawfully even on the theoretical level and indeed of course practically as well. This say in contrast to the situation of Senator and Mrs

[27] *Plato's Meno*, tr J Holbo and B Waring (2002) 44.

[28] John M Cooper and GMA Grube, *Plato: The Trial and Death of Socrates* (Hackett Publishing, 2000).

Bird who did have the choice theoretically and practically to leave their home state of Ohio if they disagree with its laws. Hence the only option left for George then is to flee towards that new life in a state (within the then United States) which was not a slave-owning State. George's determination to flee the bondage and indeed the oppression of slavery is as great and as adamant as that of Socrates's refusal under radically different circumstances to escape from prison.

To quote George again 'so that I can earn myself at least six feet of free soil—the first and last I shall ever own'. We submit that in a sense, George, the fictional runaway slave, was equally unequivocal about his preference as a free if dead man (person) as Socrates was in choosing death over submission to the injunction that he philosophised no further as a condition of *not*finding him guilty in his (Socrates) trial.[29] Socrates last words to the jury was 'O Athenians: the hour of departure has arrived, I to die and you to live, among those two paths, which is the better one, I do not know, you do not know, only the gods know'.[30] Even though Harriet Beecher Stowe's (speaking in the form of her literary character) 'George' preference to 'earn [him] self six feet of free soil instead of in slavery' is much less well-known among literati, philosophers and others throughout the ages and all over the world we submit that the sage and philosopher Plato (who after all wrote Socrates' dialogues) would or should have been impressed with George's sense of purpose and determination to be free from slavery.[31]

---

[29] See Soper (n 4).

[30] The quotation was reproduced by the Editor and co-author (Myint Zan) from his memory based on what he recalled reading in both English and Burmese translations (the Burmese translation of parts of *The Apology* was made by the late poet and scholar Zawgyi his book, in Burmese, *Introduction to Plato*, 1969). After the Editor and co-author reproduced his own recall and his 'own' translation of the last words of Socrates to the jury he did search the web and this is the last words as translated by Benjamin Jowett (1817–1893) in his translation of the *Apology* reads 'The hour of departure has arrived, and we go our ways—I to die, and you to live. Which is better God only knows'. Plato, *The Apology*, tr Benjamin Jowett (Scribner and Sons, 1871). In the translation by Hugh Treddenick, *The Last Days of Socrates*, 1954, Penguin Books, Republished Penguin classic) reads: 'Now it is time that we were going, I to die and you to live, but which of us has the happier prospect is unknown to anyone but God'. The translation by Harold North Fowler reads 'But now the time has come to go away. I go to die, and you to live; but which of us goes to the better lot, is known to none but God'. Plato, *Plato in Twelve Volumes*, tr Harold North Fowler (Harvard University Press, 1966).

[31] The last five paragraphs of the essay were entirely written by the Editor contributor while adhering substantively to the points made by the first and second authors. Significant parts of the essay were also written by the Editor and third author (Myint Zan) in order to make a smoother reading stylistically and substantively while also taking into account some of the anonymous referees' substantive comments.

Bibliography

Books

Pearson, Jim and John Robertson, *Slavery in the 19th Century* (University of California Press, 1999)
Plato, *Plato in Twelve Volumes*, tr Harold North Fowler (Harvard University Press, 1966)
Plato, *Plato in Twelve Volumes*, tr WRM Lamb (Harvard University Press 1967)
Plato, *The Last Days of Socrates*, tr H Treddenick (Penguin Classics, 2003)
Plato: The Trial and Death of Socrates, tr John M Cooper and GMA Grube (Hackett Publishing, 2000)
Rachels, James, *The Legacy of Socrates: Essays in Moral Philosophy,* Stuart Rachels (ed) (Columbia University Press 2007)
Stowe, Harriet Beecher, *Uncle Tom's Cabin* (John P Jewett & Co, 1852)

Journal Article

Soper, Philip, 'Another Look at the Crito' (1996) 41 *American Journal of Jurisprudence*
Steven Deyle, 'The Irony of Liberty: Origins of the Domestic Slave Trade' (Spring 1992) 12(1) *Journal of the Early Republic*

Web Articles

Harriet Beecher Stowe Centre, *Impact of Uncle Tom's Cabin, Slavery, and the Civil War* 11 https://www.kyrene.org/cms/lib/AZ01001083/Centricity/Domain/3828/Impact%20of%20Uncle%20Toms%20Cabin.docx
McCandless, Brandi, *Slavery's Destruction of Domestic Life in Stowe's Uncle Tom's Cabin* (April 1999) http://itech.fgcu.edu/&/issues/vol2/issue1/utc.htm
Plato's Meno, tr J Holbo and B Waring (2002) https://www.staff.ncl.ac.uk/joel.wallenberg/ContextsJoelGeoff/meno.pdf
Stowe, Harriet Beecher, *Uncle Tom's Cabin (1852), Chapter XI (In Which Property Gets into an Improper State of Mind)* http://manybooks.net/titles/stowehar203203.html

Chapter 7
Relevance of Hart-Devlin Debate in Relation to the International Criminal Court

Chong Jun Min

Abstract The publication in 1957 of the Wolfenden Commission Report on the issue of whether prostitution and homosexuality should be decriminalized in the United Kingdom engendered the Hart-Devlin debate. Albeit the debate mainly deals with the domestic legislative landscape (the United Kingdom) in the late 1950s it is far from being obsolete. The writer argues that aspects of the Hart-Devlin debate is pertinent in the implementation and -to the extent that it can be effected-enforcement of international criminal law. As pointed out by John Austin, albeit in the 1830s, international law is (also) positive morality. Austin's view informed as it is in the context of his time is based on the lack of effective sanctions to ensure uniform implementation and enforcement of international law. Still, aspects of international law in Austin's time and in the early twenty-first century is suffused with ethical and moral principles. Hart's criticism of Devlin's views and his misconception of Devlin's expositions can be discerned when aspects of the Hart-Devlin debate is applied to the international criminal law mainly in reference to the International Criminal Court. The writer submits that in the principles of international criminal law, law and morality are intertwined and inseparable especially in this age of globalization.

Keywords Hart Devlin debate · John Austin · International law as 'positive morality' · 'Consensual morality' v 'amalgamation of moralities' · International criminal court

7.1 Introduction

Hart-Devlin debate started with the publication of the *Wolfenden Report on Prostitution and Homosexuality*,[1] wherein Lord Devlin's views which he wrote in response to the Report was perceived on a continuum as nearer to 'moralism' whilst Professor Hart was closer to liberalism. Lord Devlin's position as expostulated in his essays were that 'The suppression of vice is as much the law's business as the suppression

Law firm of Messr JA Yeoh, Penang, Malaysia, junmin@jayeoh.com

[1](1957) Cmnd. 247.

M. Zan (ed.), *Legal Education and Legal Traditions: Selected Essays*, SpringerBriefs in Environment, Security, Development and Peace, https://doi.org/10.1007/978-3-030-50903-3_7

of subversive activities'.[2] Professor Hart acknowledged that there is a need for the enforcement of some morals through law, but he contended that a line should be drawn, beyond that of 'harm to others' as drawn by Mill, to that of 'paternalism', a concept which was never clearly defined by Hart.[3] Hart conceded that there is some commonly shared morality which is vital to the proper functioning of a society that needed to be enforced by the law, which he termed 'universal values'.[4]

Some would suggest that the Hart-Devlin debate is now obsolete since it started in the late 1950s. That maybe so in the domestic context in the United Kingdom, but the writer submits that this is not necessarily the case in the current global society. Though not all morals are enforced in a society, the law cannot divorce itself completely from morals. More often than not there are underlying moral principles in various laws both domestically and internationally.

7.2 Harking Back to the Nineteenth Century John Austin's Positivism

In the year 1832 when his land mark work *The Province and Function of JurisprudenceDetermined* was first published John Austin stated that:

> Positive morality, as considered without regard to its goodness or badness, might be the subject of a science closely analogous to jurisprudence... since it is only in one of its branches (namely, the law of nations or international law) that positive morality, as considered without regard to its goodness or badness, has been treated by writers in a scientific or systematic manner...
>
> ...There are laws which regard the conduct of independent political societies in their various relations to one another: Or, rather, there are laws which regard the conduct of sovereigns or supreme governments in their various relations to one another. And laws or rules of this species, which are imposed upon nations or sovereigns by opinions current amongst nations, are usually styled international law."[5]

7.3 Crimes Amenable to the Jurisdiction of the International Criminal Court

Austin is correct in categorising international law as positive morality as, in the writer's opinion, some of the bulk of international law existing even in the early twenty-first century have had their respective underlying moral principles as basis for enforcement by law.

---

[2]Patrick Devlin, *The Enforcement of Morals* (London: Oxford University Press, 1965) pp. 13–14.

[3]M.D.A. Freeman, *Lloyd's Introduction to Jurisprudence*, (Sweet & Maxwell: 2008 8th Ed.) 'The Legal Enforcement of Morality', pp. 409–412.

[4]H.L.A. Hart, *The Concept of Law* (1994), pp. 193–200.

[5]J. Austin, *The Province of Jurisprudence Determined*, ed. Hart (1954)).

To illustrate this, reference is made to the four major crimes that are within the jurisdiction of the International Criminal Court ('ICC').[6] The enforcement of law in an international society will expand the 'contours' of the Hart-Devlin debate which initially dealt only with enforcement of law in a particular country- the United Kingdom.

7.4 Hart-Devlin Debate and Its Relevance Vis-à-Vis International Criminal Court

In order to have a better understanding of the subject of the Hart-Devlin debate, it is necessary to take a closer look on its elements - laws and morals. Using Hart's concept of primitive society which according to him consist only of 'duty imposing rules', which suffers from the defects of uncertainty, is static and ineffective, we can argue that the 'duty imposing rules' forms only the basic law which is intended to ensure the security and survival of that primitive society.[7] When Hart introduced his 'power conferring rules' to cure the three defects of the primitive society, that power conferring rules itself arguably is a form of enforcement of morals of that primitive society which is intended to allow the flourishing of the community.

Hart attempted to isolate the element of morals in his rule of recognition, which he described it as purely 'neutral' and 'descriptive', as he maintained in his Postscript.[8] In doing so, Hart introduced the 'internal point of view' and 'external point of view', whereby the former is the unconditioned acceptance of a set rules as law by the officials such as judges, regardless of their personal view as to the legal validity of that law in light of morality; whereas the latter as the observation by dispassionate outsiders who do not find themselves bound by the rules, but observed that there is such a set of rules being effective in the society. But it was pointed out by Stephen Perry that if the aim of the 'rule of recognition' as put by Hart, an aim of description for accuracy, then it should also consider the divergence and disparate views about what obligations people are under, but these too can only be understood by answering the pivotal question of whether people actually are under such obligations, by which would require some moral argument and not mere description of 'how things are'.[9]

The underlying moral principles of the rule of change itself recognises the public morality of a society is mutable, thus it is necessary to have the rule to allow changes to the duty imposing rules. It is hard to see how the primitive society could have agreed on that change they wanted if according to Hart, there can only be amalgamation of moralities in a society. It is submitted that the amalgamation of moralities is the usual

[6]International Criminal Court, https://www.icc-cpi.int/resourcelibrary/official-journal/rome-statute.aspx accessed 18 August 2015.

[7]H.L.A. Hart, *The Concept of Law* (1994).

[8]Ibid., Chapter VI and Postscript.

[9]S. Perry, Hart's Methodological Positivism (as quoted in *Lloyd's Introduction to Jurisprudence*, pp. 451–481).

circumstances of a society, but when it comes to considering whether a particular moral value should be enforced by the law of that society, the people of that society will have to come together, argue it, deliberate on it, with the guidance of the elite of the society, then come to a consensus as to whether that moral should be enforced, thus forming the consensual morality as depicted by Devlin.[10]

7.4.1 *Devlin's 'Consensual Morality' and the International Criminal Court*

Both Hart and Devlin agreed that there is a basic principle of morality like that of the basic principles of natural justice, as Hart calls it, the 'universal values'. Devlin did not state that because there is public morality which is common to all, therefore the government should enforce that morality. Devlin said punishment by law is not suitable where there is no consensus as to the morals which are intended to be enforced.[11] Thus it is clear when Devlin used the notion of 'consensual morality', he meant the morality which was concluded through a thorough process like that of the deliberation of jury, where the cross-section of the society, possibly with the amalgamation of moralit(ies), have evaluated and debated. It is practically absurd to expect a society to agree unanimously on something because of differences on the level of education and exposure of each and every individual within a society.

In equating Devlin's consensual morality to unanimous morality the writer submits that Hart is distorting Devlin's exposition of the need to have consensus on the morality to be enforced by law, as that with any usual enactment of law whereby consensus (in democratic societies such as the United Kingdom where the Hart-Devlin debate emerged and in their Legislatures[12]) need to be reached before the law can be properly made enforceable in a society. What Hart suggested (perhaps and in this writer's opinion) was that the amalgamation of moralities is the state of affairs prior to the society coming to a consensual morality on certain issues. There is first the state of amalgamation of moralities in the society, and then when it comes to a practical point, they will have to agree on certain issues of morals if they want to enforce it by law, thus the outcome of the deliberation is the consensual morality of that society.

As regards the Wolfenden Commission Report and subsequent Hart-Devlin debate the majority of the commentators puts the central moral issue as whether the homosexuality should be decriminalised or not.[13] Differences of views as to whether

---

[10] P. Devlin, *The Enforcement of Morals* (London: Oxford University Press, 1965).

[11] P. Devlin,' Law, Democracy and Morality', (1962) 110 (5) *University of Pennsylvania Law Review* 635 at 639.

[12] This important substantive point is added by the Editor (Myint Zan).

[13] BBC News, '1957: Homosexuality should not be a crime', 4 September 1957, BBC Home Web Site http://news.bbc.co.uk/onthisday/hi/dates/stories/september/4/newsid_3007000/3007686.stm accessed 5 August 2015. See *Sexual* Offences Act 1967. Lord Devlin's response to the

homosexuality is morally right or morally wrong can only be expected and these differences will continue based, among others, on societies and individuals' cultural, religious and political views. Some may argue the decriminalisation of homosexuality is moving towards liberalism instead of moralism. But looking at it from the perspective of 'universal values' as agreed both by Hart and Devlin, the underlying moral principles pertaining to the decriminalisation of homosexuality can be argued is to avoid discrimination against homosexuals. Thus in actual fact of the decriminalisation of homosexuality, the lawmaker had legally enforced the morals or the principle or 'precept' of non-discrimination, which is actually moving towards moralism rather than liberalism. Using Devlin's theory, it can also be argued that the lawmakers, say, in the United Kingdom, in 1967 when, 10 years after the *WolfendenCommission Report*, Legislators decriminalised consensual, non-monetary homosexual conduct in private among adults is tantamount to implementing 'consensual morality' of non-discrimination against homosexuals.

As we move towards a broader perspective, the variety of moral values of the global society becomes more complex and as a result arguably increasing the difficulty of making (international) law(s) applicable to all or most nations. Precisely because of these increased difficulties, the Hart-Devlin debate also becomes relevant, as to how the ICC as a'lawmaker' (should) decide cases whereby its decisions can possibly have implications on not just the international landscape, but at times, domestically as well.

The Statute of Rome which is the foundational document of the International Criminal Court (ICC), has (with caveats, qualifications and exceptions claim jurisdiction[14])and has the capacity to punish four major crimes:- (a) the crime of genocide; (b) crimes against humanity; (c) war crimes; and (d) the crime of aggression.[15] The obvious underlying principles which compelled the enforcement by the 'arms' of the law so to speak for these four major crimes triable by the ICC is founded upon the global public morality, whereby Hart's amalgamation of tolerated moralities and Devlin's consensual morality is the focal lens to pin point to what extent the *international* public morality should be implemented and if possible enforced by law. This form of enforcement of morality is not only desired but is necessary to defend the peace and also to protect and preserve basic human rights in a global society.

The landscape of international law is characterised by changing or evolving moral values, which leans towards liberalism alongside of globalisation. Globalisation (not only market-wise but also in the moral even legal 'realms'[16]) is the main reason why Hart-Devlin debate is still relevant about sixty years after it began. In formulating the

---

Wolfenden Report was contained in the Maccabaean Lecture that he delivered to the British Academy in 1958. See P. Devlin, *The Enforcement of Morals*, (Oxford: University Press 1959) H.L.A. Hart, *Law, Liberty and Morality*, Stanford: University Press 1963; P. Devlin, 'Law, Democracy and Morality', (1962) 110 *University of Pennsylvania Law Review* 635; R Dworkin, 'Lord Devlin and the Enforcement of Morals', (1966) 75 *Yale Law Journal*, p. 986.

[14]This important substantive point is added by the Editor (Myint Zan).

[15]Rome Statute, http://www.icc-cpi.int/nr/rdonlyres/ea9aeff7-5752-4f84-be94-0a655eb30e16/0/rome_statute_ english.pdf accessed 18 August 2015.

[16]This substantive point is added by the Editor (Myint Zan).

punishable crimes in the ICC, a consensual morality as depicted by Devlin would have taken place whereby a group of selected (appointed or elected) persons contributed a sufficient standard of contemporary morality to assess the extent of legal intervention in a tug war between the two extreme ends of liberalism and moralism.

Hart's concern lies in the unanimous consensual morality which according to him is impossible to achieve, and argued that the only possible scenario would only be an 'amalgamation of tolerated moralities', whereby the majority's perception of moral values will be enforced, whilst the minority will have to tolerate with that majority's morality. Hart argued that it is dangerous if we follow populism which contain risks for the democracy of a society. According to Hart, populism could eventually lead to majority dictatorship.[17] Hart strongly argued that that the state should not legitimately enforce morals in such a way.

Hart's concern can arguably be seen in the application of *European Convention on Human Rights* ('ECHR')[18] which is very much concerned with the individual's basic human rights, such as that of right to respect for private and family life,[19] where the public authority should not interfere in a person's private life unless for the protection of morals. A pertinent query is, to what extent does the ECHR means by 'morals'? Hart would argue that if no harms were done to the society, then it is no value in using the threats to enforce the morals through the law.[20] Whereas Devlin would disagree by saying that 'immorality' itself is a necessary and sufficient condition for criminalisation: there is no need to consider the issue of whether the act itself is causing harm to the others or not.[21]

Hart by limiting the enforcement of morals to situations where the society would be harmed as propounded by Mill and for paternalism could limit the society's improvement as a whole. Using the example of International Criminal Court and *European Convention of Human Rights* ('ECHR'), the ICC as the international court can be considered to be implementing the 'morals' of international society will have to observe namely the consensual morality of the global society, whereby it is commonly agreed that the crime of genocide, crime against humanity, war crimes and crime of aggression is morally wrong. The writer would argue that enforcement of morals in this case is in accord with Devlin's consensual morality. Hart may argue that in the case of ECHR, the member state, such as United Kingdom, did not incorporate the whole of the ECHR into their domestic law. Still, it is hard to see how the argument of amalgamation of moralities can fit properly in this particular example.

Arguably, the whole of the ECHR has the global or (at least European public morality[22]) as its base, and each of the rights and prohibitions entrenched has their

---

[17] H.L.A. Hart, *Law, Liberty and Morality* (New York: Vintage Books, 1963).

[18] *European Convention on Human Rights*, http://www.echr.coe.int/Documents/Convention_ENG.pdf.

[19] *European Convention on Human Rights*, Article 8.

[20] Michael D. Bayles, *Hart's Legal Philosophy: An Examination* (1992) pp 205.

[21] Russell Sandberg Anonimo, '*Criminal*', Routledge-Cavendish: 2008, p. 113.

[22] This important substantive point is added by the Editor (Myint Zan).

respective underlying moral principles within it. Albeit certain countries may not completely agree with all the human rights stated therein, it is almost certain none of a legitimate political sovereign would disagree with it completely and reject all of the rights and prohibitions. Instead of labelling such a situation as 'amalgamation of tolerated moralities' as Hart suggests, it is proposed that it would be better termed as 'qualified consensual morality', because to certain extent, some level of consensus has been met.

7.4.2 Consensual Morality and Implementation of International Judicial Decisions

Article 53 of the *1969 Vienna Convention on Treaties* provides that a treaty is void if it conflicts with a 'peremptory norm of general international law', which was also defined therein as a norm accepted and recognised by the international community of States as a whole as a norm from which no derogation is permitted and which can be modified only by a subsequent norm of general international law having the same character.[23] Basically these norms are also known as *jus cogens* which are almost equivalent to that of international constitutional importance as a body of principles accepted by the international society collectively to ensure that no treaty could override it.[24] A peremptory norm of international law (*jus cogens*) prohibits the unlawful threat or use of force, genocide, slavery or piracy which is essentially the enforcement of morality by law and international ethics among sovereign States.

The enforcement of international law has always been questioned by many scholars principally because of the defect rightly identified by Austin, that it lacks the element of sanctions. This is recently illustrated in China's refusal to submit and abide by the rulings of the Permanent Court of Arbitration at Hague in The South China Sea Arbitration, which was initiated by the Republic of the Philippines.[25] The best argument to support the contention that China should abide by international law would be none other than of the need to enforce morality, in order to maintain the peace and harmonious relationship amongst other sovereign States.

Applying Hart's argument in this scenario, assuming China as an individual in a global society, the enforcement of morality should be only to prevent harm to others in the global society and for paternalism to prevent the harm to the individual itself. Applying Hart's standpoint (albeit initially made domestically in relation to the United Kingdom) 'international morality' (abiding by decisions of courts or tribunals

---

[23] *Vienna Convention on the Law of Treaties* (with annex), concluded at Vienna on 23 May 1969. https://treaties.un.org/doc/Publication/UNTS/Volume%201155/volume-1155-I-18232-English.pdf.

[24] A. Cassese, *International* law, (Oxford: Oxford University Press, 2005) 2nd Ed, Chapter 11:' The *hierarchy of rules in international law: the role of juscogens*', pp. 201–212.

[25] *The Republic of the Philippines v The People's Republic of China*, The South China Sea Arbitration, The Hague Press Release, 12 July 2016.

which the State parties *apriori* have agreed to submit and also agreed to abide by their decisions) should be implemented even enforced by international law -should there at all possible- at least In a few cases it may not be possible![26] The rationale for such enforcement from a Hartian perspective so to speak would be that there is a need to prevent (arguable) 'harm' or at least negatively effect the rights of an 'entity' namely the State of Philippines (which strictly speaking is neither an individual nor a society in the Hartian or Devlinian sense.)[27] Applying Devlin's thesis to the Philippines-China imbroglio it is arguable that the very act by China in ignoring or defying not to abide by the arbitral decision is a (moral) and on the theoretical level legal justification to 'enforce' (international morality (it might again be added) if it is at all possible in this particular case![28]

7.5 Conclusion

The writer submits that international law is the very subject where laws and morals are intertwined and are inseparable. The debate of enforcement of morals and morality will continue for many more years to come and, in the light of globalisation, can hardly be seen as obsolete. The constant question is 'Where is/are the line(s) to be drawn?' Both Hart and Devlin's contentions will continue to serve as lighthouses on different shores to guide the lawmakers both domestically and internationally to decide on these issues. What is certain is that nothing can be achieved without the consensual morality among the parties concerned in the global arena. The Hart-Devlin debate is very much alive and is relevant for the safety and betterment of the international society.

Bibliography

Books

Annimo, Russell Sandberg, 'Criminal', Routledge-Cavendish: (2008)
Austin, J *The Province of Jurisprudence Determined*, (ed. Hart (1954)
Cassese, A. *International Law*, (Oxford: Oxford University Press, 20052nd Ed)
H.L.A. Hart, *Law, Liberty and Morality*, (New York: Vintage Books, 1963)
Bayles, Michael D, *Hart's Legal Philosophy: An Examination* (1992)
Devlin, Patrick, *The Enforcement of Morals* (London: Oxford University Press, 1965)
Freeman, M.D.A. *Lloyd's Introduction to Jurisprudence*, (Sweet & Maxwell: 2008 8th Ed.)
Hart, H.L.A, *The Concept of Law* (Oxford University Press, 1994)

---

[26] This important substantive point is added by the Editor (Myint Zan).
[27] This substantive point is added by the Editor (Myint Zan).
[28] Added by the Editor (Myint Zan).

Legislation

Sexual Offences Act, 1967 (United Kingdom)

International Conventions

European Convention on Human Rights, http://www.echr.coe.int/Documents/Convention_ENG.pdf
Vienna Convention on the Law of Treaties (with annex), concluded at Vienna on 23 May 1969 https://www.jus.uio.no/lm/un.law.of.treaties.convention.1969/
Statute of the International Criminal Court, Rome Statute, http://www.icc-cpi.int/nr/rdonlyres/ea9aeff7-5752-4f84-be94-0a655eb30e16/0/rome_statute_english.pdf

Case

The Republic of the Philippines v The People's Republic of China, The South China Sea Arbitration, The Hague Press Release , 12 July 2016

Articles

Devlin, P 'Law, Democracy and Morality', (1962) 110 (5) *University of Pennsylvania Law Review* 635
Dworkin, R 'Lord Devlin and the Enforcement of Morals', (1996) *75 Yale Law Journal*

Others

Wolfenden Report on Prostitution and Homosexuality (1957) Cmnd. 247
BBC News, '1957: Homosexuality should not be a crime', 4 September 1957, BBC Home Web Site http://news.bbc.co.uk/onthisday/hi/dates/stories/september/4/newsid_3007000/3007686.stm

Chapter 8
Spillover Thoughts in Rereading Time's Magazine's Obituary of Historian Arnold Toynbee: Teleologies of History, Contingency and *Sub Specie Aeternitatis*

Myint Zan

Abstract The first part of this chapter analyses what historian of human civilizations Arnold Toynbee would have thought and said of the Stephen Jay Gould and Simon Conway Morris debate regarding the Burgess Shale in relation to contingency (Gould's point) and teleology (Conway Morris'). In addition, the views regarding the teleological interpretation of human history discernible in the Christian and Marxian 'triumphalism' of Saint Augustine and Karl Marx's philosophies of history are also analysed. The views of the evolutionist and historian of science Ernst Mayr on the contingency/teleology debate are noted. The second part canvasses and juxtaposes the seventeenth century philosopher Spinoza's *sub specie aeternitatis* with those of Toynbee's exhortation to overcome 'intellectual provincialism' in viewing 'human affairs'. Contemporary notions (in some circles) of (Intelligent) Design, Consilience and Emergence/Fine-tuning are also analysed from what the author of the Chapter considered to be Spinozist viewpoints.

Keywords Arnold Toynbee · Augustine · Karl Marx · Debate between Stephen Jay Gould and Simon Conway Morris regarding Burgess Shale · Ernst Mayr · Spinoza · Contingency · Teleology · *Sub specie aeternitatis*

8.1 Introduction

The historian Arnold J. Toynbee (14 April 1889–22 October 1975) died in October 1975. *Time* magazine published an obituary about Arnold Toynbee in its 3 November

Myint Zan, former (until December 2016) Professor Faculty of Law, Multimedia University, Malacca, Malaysia. Email: myintzan@yahoo.com.au.

The author dedicates this essay to the memory of his late parents Dr. San Baw (29 June 1922–7 December 1984) and Professor Dr Myint MyintKhin (15 December 1923–19 June 2014) who 'notes' the interest of their son on things philosophical and, at times, encourage his interest in philosophy.

M. Zan (ed.), *Legal Education and Legal Traditions: Selected Essays*,
SpringerBriefs in Environment, Security, Development and Peace,
https://doi.org/10.1007/978-3-030-50903-3_8

1975 issue.[1] By chance or perhaps by (unintended?) design[2] the author has re-read it several times. The concluding sentences of the obituary read:

> Daniel Boorstin, recently confirmed as the new Librarian of Congress, commented that "few historians have spent themselves so unstintingly or so effectively in the effort to transcend the provincialism of their time and place." Toynbee felt that there was a kind of intellectual provincialism, too, in what he called "the dogma that 'life is just one damned thing after another,'" for he himself had "a lifetime conviction that human affairs do not become intelligible until they are seen as a whole."

This chapter is divided into a few parts:

- First, an excursus about other theories or what can be described as teleological view of history.
- Second, the nature of natural (non-human) history and the debate between the late Stephen Jay Gould and Simon Conway Morris on whether evolutionary history is contingent (a general proposition of Gould) and 'convergent' or as will be elaborated later 'teleological' (that of Conway Morris). In the latter part of this section what Toynbee would have commented on the debate between the contingent and convergent views of natural history would be explored in Part I of the Chapter.
- Part II would be a comment on the statement regarding 'intellectual provincialism' and that 'human affairs (becoming) intelligible only when they are seen as a whole' mainly from what this author considers to be a Spinozist perspective.

Part I: Teleological Views on Human and Natural History: Toynbee's Possible View On the Gould-Conway Morris Debate

8.2 Earlier Teleological Views of (Human) History: Augustine and Marx

Toynbee's view of history as possibly having a teleological, purpose-driven approach of and analysis of history can also be found in a few other ideologies or philosophies.

Marxists also believe there is a 'force' in history called historical materialism[3] which according to them moves toward the (almost pre-determined end) of history:

[1]*Time,* 'Education: Vision of God's Creation', 3 November 1975.

[2]Generally the philosophical implication of the word 'design' includes both a 'designer' and/or 'intention' or purpose. Stephen Hawking and Leonard Mlodinow, *The Grand Design* (Bantam 2010). Though the word 'design' was used in the title of their book Hawking and Mlodinow reject the idea of a designer or to be more explicit Creator of the Universe. See also part II text and notes accompanying notes 103 to 110.

[3]See, eg, Karl Marx, *A Contribution to the Critique of Political Economy* (republication 1977, Moscow Progress Publishers, notes by R Rojas) *par tim.* Among many others critiques of historical materialism see Karl Popper, *Conjectures and Refutations*: *The Growth of Scientific Knowledge* (Routledge 2003, first published in 1963) *par tim.* For a relatively recent defence of Marxism see Terry Eagleton, *Why Marx Was Right* (Yale University Press, 2011).

apparently the triumph of socialism and communism over that of capitalism.[4] Many centuries before Karl Marx, the Christian philosophers St. Augustine and St. Thomas Aquinas (these two Christian philosophers lived and died more than 800 years apart) had espoused their views based on their own theologies and they can be described as the teleological interpretations of history.[5] Augustine's and Aquinas' view was influenced if not inspired, in part, by the Greek philosopher Aristotle's views on teleology.

Just as Karl Marx, in the mid-to late nineteenth century, wrongly(so far) 'predicted' the down fall of capitalism and the (eventual) triumph of socialism and communism Augustine had about 1400 years earlier asserted that at the end of history there will be eternal punishment of the 'damned'.[6] Augustine also wrote about 'the eternal happiness of the saints' at the end of *The City of God.*[7] Therefore at least in the generalized sense of the word it is perhaps not altogether inappropriate to consider that Augustine's – and about fourteen centuries later – Marx's view of history as being purpose-driven and pre-determined has (varying) shades of the teleological views of history.

8.3 Gould and Conway Morris' Debate on the Nature of Evolutionary History

In the last quarter of the twentieth century less than 15 years after Toynbee died the late Stephen Jay Gould argued in his book *Wonderful Life: The Burgess Shale and the Nature of History* (first published 1989)[8] that deals with the Burgess Shale (which is now located in the Canadian Rockies in British Columbia) of a period of about 505–520 million years ago. The sub-title of Gould's book explicitly deals with the 'nature of *history*': 'Replay the tape of life' wrote Gould '"a million times" from a Burgess beginning, and I doubt that anything like homo sapiens would ever evolve again'.[9]

---

[4]Contrary to what Marx had predicted and many Marxists the world over hoped for history has not moved towards the triumph of socialism. The past few decades had witnessed the dominance and triumph of capitalism in most parts of the world. See, e.g., Meghnad Desai: *Marx's Revenge: The Resurgence of Capitalism and the Death of Statist Socialism* (Verso, 2004).

[5]For Augustine's view of history see among others, his *The City of God Against the Pagans,* tr RW Dyson (Cambridge University Press, 1998), Books V, XI,XV, XX, XX. *par tim.*

[6]See, eg, ibid, book XXI.

[7]See, eg, ibid, book XXII.

[8]Stephen Jay Gould, *Wonderful Life: The Burgess Shale and the Nature of History* (WW Norton and Company, 1989).

[9]Ibid 289.

8.3.1 *Gould's 'Rewinding the Tape of Life' and Conway Morris' 'Trivia'*

One of the 'heroes'[10] of Gould's book Simon Conway Morris rebutted Gould in his own book *The Crucible of Creation: Burgess Shale and the Rise of Animals* first published in 1998 that it is inevitable that human like creatures would eventually arise[11] and that Gould's postulation is 'trivial'. However the example of 'triviality' given by Conway Morris himself seems to this writer, to be quite trivial. Conway Morris writes:

> ... let me explain why I think that the metaphor of rerunning the tape of life is rather trivial. Viewed biologically, one hundred years ago my existence would have been inconceivable other than that perhaps as the fond but hypothetical musings of my grandparents. If my parents had not met, the world would be full of humans, but I would not be writing these words. But it is worse than that. If my parents had not made love on a particular day in early February 1950[12] again I would not be here. Their child conceived on another occasion, would certainly be similar to me, but distinguishable in all the ways that brothers and sisters differ.[13]

Whereas Conway Morris went only about as far as '100 years ago' Gould in contrast goes back (literally) hundreds of millions of years further into the past all the way back to the Burgess shale animal *Pikaia* who had 'survived the Burgess decimation' about 520 million years ago.[14]

---

[10]Gould has been very generous in his praise of the pioneering work done by the late Harry Whitington (1916–2010), Derek Briggs and Simon Conway Morris throughout the book in regard to reinterpreting the significance of the fossils of the Burgess Shale.

[11]See, e.g., *The Crucible of Creation*, 138–139, 199–221. See also Simon Conway Morris, *Life's Solution: Inevitable Humans in a Lonely Universe* (Cambridge University Press, 2004) It is not unusual in other disciplines other than paleobiology (*Wonderful Life* v *Crucible of Creation*) to have books and articles published in 'response ' so to speak. For example, in the field of social science and political philosophy Robert Nozick's, *Anarchy, State and Utopia* (1974) can be considered to be published, in part, as a response to and which challenged the premises of the earlier work of Nozick's Harvard colleague John Rawls, *A Theory of Justice* (Harvard University Press, 1971). About a decade earlier Lon Fuller's *The Morality of Law* (Yale University Press, 1964) was written at least partly if not largely in response to HLA Hart's *The Concept of Law* (Clarendon Press, 1st ed, 1961). For an early twenty-first century narration and retrospective of the Hart-Fuller debate on legal positivism see, Nicola Lacey, 'Out of the "Witches" Cauldron? Reinterpreting the Context and Reassessing the Significance of the Hart-Fuller Debate' in Peter Cane (ed), *The Hart-Fuller Debate in the Twenty-First Century* (Hart Publishing, 2010). See also and compare Julius Stone, *Israel and Palestine, An Assault on the Law of Nations* (Johns Hopkins University Press, 1982) with John B Quigley, *Palestine and Israel, A Challenge to Justice* (Duke University Press, 1990).

[12]The *Wikipedia* article on Simon Conway Morris states that he was 'born on 6 November 1951' https://en.wikipedia.org/wiki/Simon_Conway_Morris (accessed 28 April 2011). Coming from the protagonist writing about himself Conway Morris would have been born not in November 1951 but in November 1950. Again quoting Conway Morris own reasoning the individual born in November 1951(as a result of his parents' love-making in February *1951* instead of February 1950) would not have been the individual whose writings I am commenting on but could be 'distinguishable [from Conway Morris] in all the ways that brothers and sisters differ'.

[13]Morris (n 12) at 201.

[14]Writes Gould:

Conway's Morris description of Gould's 'grand claim' or to borrow a title from one of the late Francis Crick's books 'astonishing hypothesis[15]' as 'trivial' is shared (and though he did not use the same word) by Daniel Dennett of Tufts University in his book *Darwin's Dangerous Idea.*[16] Dennett was equally critical of Gould's postulates and arguments about 'rewinding the tape of life'. Simon Conway Morris and Daniel Dennett's theology[17] philosophy and views on evolutionary theory could be hardly more different in many significant aspects but they seem to write almost in unison in making light of or dismissing Gould's admittedly *not* 'falsifiable' thesis.

And so if you wish to ask the question of the ages-why do humans exist? A major part of the answer, touching those aspects of the issue that science can treat at all, must be because *Pikaia* survived the Burgess decimation. This does not cite a single law of nature, it embodies *no statement of predictable evolutionary pathways*, no calculation of probabilities based on general rules of anatomy or ecology. The survival of *Pikaia*was a contingency of "just history". I do not think that any higher answer can be given and I cannot imagine that any resolution could be more fascinating.' (Gould n 9) (emphasis added).

Gould's statement emphasised above differs from that the historians or philosophies of history espoused by Aristotle, Augustine, Aquinas, and Marx where bold predictions of the pathways of history (albeit human history) were made. In the case of Augustine and Aquinas the pathways were (and are) divinely inspired or even commanded by the (Christian) God; in the case of Marx they were dialectically and materialistically guided.

[15]Francis Crick, *Astonishing Hypothesis: The Scientific Search for the Soul* (Scribner, 1995). From this writer's understanding through reading both books by Crick and Gould Crick's exposition and location of the soul may be untestable and perhaps (arguably) may or may not be falsifiable but it is not as fanciful as that of Gould.

[16]Daniel Dennett, *Darwin's Dangerous Idea*, Chapter 10, is entitled 'Bully for Brontosaurus' and is mainly a refutation of Gould's theses by Dennett which runs from pages 262 to 312. The sub-title 'Tinker to Evers to Chance: The Burgess Shale Double Play Mystery' (pages 299–311) is devoted to debunking Gould's, (in Dennett's phrase 'The Boy Who Cried Wolf'), views on the Burgess Shale animals and the course of history.

[17]See, eg, his statement that "the scientist who boomingly—and they always boom—declares that those who believe in the Deity are unavoidably crazy, 'cracked' as my dear father would have said, although I should add that I have every reason to believe he was—and now hope is—on the side of the angels" (Boyle's Lecture, 2005, 'Darwin's Compass; How Evolution Discovers the Song of Creation' https://www.giffordlectures.org/lectures/darwins-compass-how-evolution-discovers-song-creation (16 June 2011). Hence there is an implicit belief in or at least metaphorical mention of 'angels' – and inasmuch as a theological grounding has to be made they would be that of the Christian angels. Even shorn of its theological connotations contrast Conway Morris' explicit assertion that he and his late father's are on the side of the angels (the 'eventual' winners in the 'song of creation') with his sneering tone against his ideological adversaries the Marxists whose views he dismissively wrote are 'principally linked to certain inevitable outcomes that strangely favoured

8.3.1.1 'Coffin of Atheism', Marxist (and Christian) Agendas

It can be described that Conway Morris is at the least a theist if not a Christian (Anglican) theist for that matter.[18] Conway Morris writes that 'Darwinism has reached near saturation and among the customary pieties there is little doubt that it will conveniently served as a little love-in, with much mutual self-congratulation for atheism'.[19] Conway Morris rhetorically asks 'Isn't it curious how evolution is regarded by some as a total, universe embracing solution[20] although those who treat it as a religion might protest some times not gently'.[21] Conway Morris adds 'interestingly and unsurprisingly'[22] that 'Don't worry the science of evolution is certainly

---

those fortunate enough to have formulated them in the first place'. Indeed. Conway Morris' Lecture on evolution whose sub-title is 'The Song of Creation' 'hopes' that 'eventual outcome' of the debate as to the pathways of evolution would favour those who had similar views like those of himself and late father and who 'are fortunate enough to have formulated them'.

[18] See, eg, Simon Conway Morris, 'Darwin was right. Up to a point', *The Guardian*, 12 February 2009. The article was published 'designedly' (both by the writer and editors), it can be said with confidence, on the 200th anniversary of the birth of Charles Darwin.

[19] Ibid.

[20] Footnote inserted. Though no where in his article Daniel Dennett's name is mentioned one wonders one of the unnamed targets of Conway Morris' critiques is Dennett who uses the term 'universal acid' (see, eg, 'Universal Acid: Handle with Care') to describe Darwinism in *Darwin's Dangerous idea.*

[21] Ibid.

[22] The late Mr. Justice Scalia of the United States Supreme Court in the case of *Crosby v National Foreign Trade Council* 530 US 363, 388–391 (2000) decided on 19 June 2000, the learned Justice (interestingly) use the phrase 'interesting (albeit unsurprising)' one, two, three, four times in a four page concurring opinion where Scalia 'concurred only in the judgment' of a unanimous court decision. The Supreme Court held that 'the Burma law of the Commonwealth of Massachusetts restricting the authority of its agencies to purchase goods and services from companies doing business with Burma is invalid under the Supremacy Clause of the National Constitution'. Ibid 363. Scalia was being ironic in critiquing and –as was his wont- deriding the reasoning of the opinion of Justice Souter joined by six other Justices which make use of legislative history in coming to their decision as 'interesting (albeit) unsurprising'. Lest the reader thinks that this writer's 'excursus' (a term which –again-Justice Scalia used in his concurring opinion with a tone of derision, see ibid 389) into a concurring opinion of a United States Supreme Court Justice is (in the words of Justice Scalia himself ibid 391) an exercise in 'persistent irrelevancy' he would point out 'in mitigation' that Mr. Justice Scalia was in the *Crosby* case dealing with a comparable subject to this article namely (legislative) history and he had had his 'excurses' into the subject of evolution history in terms of his wrong-headed views (in this author's opinion) in Scalia's dissenting opinion (exactly thirteen years to the day on 19 June 1987 before his concurring judgment in *Crosby* decided on 19 June 2000, from the holding in the case of *Edwards v Aguillard*, 482 US 578 (1987). In *Edwards v Aguillard*it was held that a Louisiana (state) law requiring that creation science be taught in public schools along with evolution was unconstitutional because the law was specifically intended to

incomplete'[23]Conway Morris ends his article indeed in a very 'complete', overtly (over) confident and snide manner with these words:

> Of course our brains are a product of evolution, but does anybody seriously believe consciousness itself is material? Well, yes, some argue just as much,[24] but their explanations seem to have made no headway. We are indeed dealing with unfinished business. God's funeral? I don't think so. Please join me beside the coffin marked Atheism. I fear, however, there will be very few mourners.[25]

There are similar smug phrases in *The Crucible of Creation* where almost *ad hominem* attacks on atheism as well as Marxism (on a philosophical level, atheism and Marxism, at least in certain contexts, are mutually exclusive)[26] are made. Conway Morris wrote in effect that the whole thesis of Gould reflected 'a particular world-view that at the least was sympathetic to the greatest of twentieth-century pseudo-religions: Marxism'.[27]

What is (or in this it should probably be was since Gould has been dead since May 2002) sauce for the goose should be sauce for the gander as well. Isn't Conway Morris view also influenced by his belief (sophisticated no doubt and 'spruced up' no doubt by his impressive and – in regards to the initial work done at the Burgess shale – sterling paleontological and scientific credentials) in Christianity? Conway Morris states that Gould's views reflects the 'Marxist agenda' which 'has long sought 'laws' of history, principally linked to certain inevitable outcomes that strangely favoured those fortunate enough to have formulated them in the first place'.[28]As pointed out earlier, it is not only in the 'agenda' or in the Marxist view of history that 'inevitable' out comes are predicted and also to those who favoured their 'side'. Augustine who preceded Marx by 1400 years also had his own view of history which favour[ed] (again) 'interestingly' albeit unsurprisingly the Christians.[29]

promote ideas pertaining to religion. For a compelling critique of Scalia's dissenting opinion see Stephen Jay Gould, 'Justice Scalia's Misunderstanding' (1987) 87 *Natural History* 137–140.

[23]Morris (n 19).

[24]One philosopher who did argue that (for want of a better word and to simplify for the sake of brevity) that 'consciousness is material' 'just as much' is Daniel Dennett. See Daniel Dennett, *Consciousness Explained* (Black Bay Book, 1992).

[25]Morris (n 19).

[26]See, eg, the writings of the anti-Marxist, anti-Communist but atheist Ayn Rand's writings especially *Atlas Shrugged* (first published, 1957).Compare to Ayn Rand an atheist with right-wing political views Bertrand Russell can be considered if not to the political 'left' then at least not that right-wing. Russell too had criticized Christianity 'Why I am Not a Christian' (first published as a book let around 1927) and Communism. 'Why I am not a Communist' (first published in 1956).

[27]Morris (n 12) 7.

[28]Ibid 11–12.

[29]See, eg, Augustine (n 5).

8.3.2 *Falsifiability of the Cause of Dinosaur Extinction and Unfalsifiability of Gould and Conway Morris Thesis?*

The statement that both Gould's and Conway Morris' postulates about (not) rerunning the 'tape of life' and seeing whether or not humans will arise in the process of evolution is not falsifiable need some elaboration. The fact is one cannot re-run history. Gould may be accused of hyperbole whenhe states that 'rerun the tape of life a million times' human like creatures would not arise again. Conway Morris argues that 'rerun the tape of life as many times as you like' human like creatures would appear again. Since the tape of life cannot be re-run even once it would *prima facie* seem that both Gould's and Conway Morris' claims would be equally unfalsifiable.

Falsification of (scientific) hypothesis can also be effected in scientific disciplines which is not amenable to the empirical method: disciplines known as the historical sciences. For example, the major cause for the extinction of dinosaurs as a result of asteroid hitting the Yucatan peninsular[30] around 65 million years ago cannot be re-enacted even once. Still, the 'proof' or veracity of this asteroid of 65 million years ago being the major cause of the extinction of the dinosaurs is now a very strong hypothesis.[31] Unlike the existence of gravity which can be 'proven' by way of experiment (dropping objects on Earth) 'a million times' such a repeat method of 'verification' of a hypothesis is not possible in the case, one submits, of both Gould's and Conway Morris' postulations. Even though Conway Morris has stated that Gould's idea of 'rewinding the tape of life' is trivial he had also asserted that the rise of human intelligence and humans are inevitable.[32]

To a lay but interested person like this writer the hypotheses of overwhelming unlikeliness of human types creatures emerging should the 'tape of life' be 're-run' (Gould) and the virtual inevitable emergence of 'human like intelligence' (Conway Morris) is both unfalsifiable. It is realised that Conway Morris has stated that Gould's metaphor or 'construct' of 'rerunning the tape of life' 'misses the point',[33] is 'trivial'[34]

---

[30]For the first formulation of this hypothesis see Luis W Alvarez, et al., 'Extraterrestrial Cause for the Cretaceous–Tertiary Extinction' (1980) 208(4448) *Science* 1095–1108.

[31]More than thirty years after the hypothesis was first proposed there are further strong supporting evidence for such a hypothesis, see, eg, P. Claeys and S. Goderis 'Solar System: Lethal Billiards' (2007) 449(7158) *Nature* 30–31. For a contemporaneous report of further (a few may say 'clinching') evidence that the asteroid caused the extinction of the dinosaurs see Tyler R. Lyson, et al., 'Dinosaur Extinction: Closing the "3 m gap"' (July 13, 2011) 7 *Biology Letters*, doi: 10.1098/rsbl.2011.0470, (accessed 15 July 2011).

[32]In his debate with Gould in *Natural History* magazine, (1998) (107) (10) p 48 Conway Morris writes: 'I believe that a creature with intelligence and self-awareness on a level with our own would surely have evolved—although perhaps not from a tailless, upright ape. Almost any planet with life, in my view, will produce living creatures we would recognize as parallel in form and function to our own biota'.com.

[33]Morris (n 12) 201.

[34]Ibid 206.

or 'simply incorrect or uninteresting'.[35] Yet one submits at least the abstract and of the first part of Simon Conway Morriss' Gifford Lecture[36] also has to play the Gouldian game, so to speak, of 're-running the tape of life'. The gist of the Lecture has a bearing on the dichotomy of the extreme improbability v near inevitability of humans like creatures or intelligence arising or not as a result of the evolutionary process.

The falsifiability or indeed testability in the historical sciences is not the same as in the physical sciences as simply but effectively pointed out by the late Arthur C. Clarke in a brief but compelling Letter to the Editor that was published in *Time* magazine in June 1983. When a reader writes to *Time*'s editors in response to an article about Stephen Jay Gould a reader writes that 'Gould should know that a basic tenet of scientific method is that phenomena must be repeatable and verifiable through observation. The law of gravity is easily verifiable; the concept of evolution remains only a theory precisely because it cannot be repeated and verified through observation'.[37] To which Arthur C. Clarke's replies:

Reader Charles Beck's letter [June 20] criticizes the acceptance of evolution as a phenomenon because it is not "repeatable and verifiable." Neither is the entire historical record. Does Beck really doubt that George Washington or Jesus Christ ever lived? The evidence for the fact (not theory!) of evolution is far stronger than for the existence of Jesus, though not quite as good as for that of Washington's.[38]

The difference between the historical sciences and the physical sciences which 'reader Charles Beck' confuses should be clear enough. It is perhaps also applicable to events that are not repeatable and verifiable like the extinction of the dinosaurs where 'the tape of life' could not be rewind again. Yet its factual occurrence can be if not 'proven' strongly inferable through the historical evidence. As for the 'rewinding the tape of life' which deals not with a historical evidence on what had actually happened –or not- but what might had and what it could lead to is a different matter. Despite the best efforts of Gould and Conway Morris, for this dilettante, no definitive conclusion can be derived as to whether human intelligence would arise or not since humans had only (historically) evolved only once.

---

[35]Ibid 199.

[36]The Gifford Lectures by Simon Conway Morris were delivered in six parts and 'Lecture One' entitled 'Life's Solution: The Predictability of Evolution across the Galaxy (and Beyond)' was delivered on 19 February 2007.

[37]Letters to the Editor by Charles Beck, Dover Air Force Base, Del[aware], under the Section 'Iconoclastic Scientist', (*Time* magazine) June 20, 1983. Beck was commenting on an article about Stephen Jay Gould entitled 'Science: Bone, Baseball and Evolution' and apparently responding to Gould's statement that 'evolution is only a theory, where Gould 'retorts that 'Nonsense. Evolution is as real as gravity. Whether you believe in Newton's, Einstein's or someone else explanation of it, the apple still falls'.

[38]Letters to the Editor by Arthur C. Clarke, Colombo, Sri Lanka, under the Section 'Iconoclastic Scientist' (Time), July 18, 1983.

8.3.3 Toynbee on the Gould Conway Morris Debate

Since this Chapter starts with Toynbee's view of history it would now consider what would Toynbee have said to Gould's and Conway Morris views on history even if they are not about human history. This question is pertinent since in his life-time Toynbee 'had become an international sage, like Einstein, Schweitzer or Bertrand Russell, who was asked for his opinion on all manner of subjects'.[39]

True, Toynbee's expertise was on human history but as stated previously the writings of Gould in *Wonderful Life* deals specifically with *the nature of history* being a sub-title of the book. And the nature of history is a topic well within Toynbee's expertise. As stated earlier it could be queried whether Toynbee's view of history has affinities with the ancient Greek philosopher Aristotle's view about *telos* or purpose or that of the medieval philosopher Augustine. The author will not try to answer that query beyond pointing to the fact that Aristotle's purpose or 'God' (if you will) as the 'unmoved mover' is quite different from the Christian God of Augustine.

Time's magazine obituary situates Toynbee's work in the context of the 'Vision of God's Creation'. Perhaps it can be inferred that the process of history can be viewed if not in terms of a 'goal' or a teleology then at least in terms of an unfolding perhaps directed or 'designed' by God. It is noteworthy that both Toynbee's obituary in *Time* and Conway Morris' book *The Crucible of Creation: Burgess Shale and the Rise of Animals* use the word 'Creation'. Moreover a certain curial perspective (indeed vision) is inherent in the description of the life work of Toynbee's apparent philosophy of history embodied as it were that history is a *vision* of God's Creation. Hence the pertinent question: would Toynbee have agreed with Conway Morris's view, perhaps a grander or – at least much (much) longer-view of natural history[40] which eventually led to 'inevitable humans' albeit 'in a lonely universe' and thereafter to the unfolding of human history.

The question that arises considering (for the purpose of this query) that the Gould-Conway Morris debate was about the nature of history (albeit events stretching over

[39] *Time* (n 1).

[40] The word 'grander' is used in the sense that where Toynbee's copious output of the rise and fall of civilizations in human history is indeed grand and sweeping, Conway Morris is even more so 'grand' (albeit in the not so grand sense of the word) in that it deals long before humans and their history arise and the 'inevitability' of humans arising.

scores of millions of years resulting in the emergence of humans) is about 'contingency' as stated by Gould[41] and 'convergence' as espoused by Conway Morris,[42] which view of history in general would Toynbee agree more with?

One could foresee a possible 'objection' to be raised here: that this exercise is (to quote Conway Morris' ingratiating or at least ironic reference to Gould's 'metaphor' of replaying the tape of life) 'trivial'.[43] Toynbee has been dead for more than a dozen years when Gould first published his *Wonderful Life* in 1989 and it was in 1998 that Conway Morris' response to Gould in the form of *The Crucible of Creation* was first published when Toynbee would have been 109 years old.[44] Yet analyses of and *a posterori* commentaries on two legal scholars' 'argument' on an aspect of legal philosophy in a famous debate in another academic discipline have been canvassed in the form of a book of essays published in the year 2010 more than fifty years after academic journal articles on the topic of debate was first published.[45] Similarly it is a valid academic exercise to attempt to 'gauge' what a personage in what can be said to be a 'social science' discipline or that of the humanities[46] (Arnold Toynbee as a

---

[41]See, eg, the last Chapter of *Wonderful Life* the heading of which reads, 'Possible Worlds: The Power of Just History' (Chapter V). The immediate subheading of the Chapter reads 'A Story of Alternatives' (pp. 292–299) and the next sub-heading reads 'General Patterns that Illustrate Contingency' (pp. 299-308). In the following section 'Seven Possible Worlds' Gould writes about ' … biology's most profound insight into human nature, status and potential lies in the simple phrase, the embodiment of contingency. Homo Sapiens is an entity not a tendency. By taking this form of argument across all scales of time and extent, and right to the heart of our own evolution, *I hope I have convinced you that contingency matters where it counts most.*' (Emphasis added). It is 'clear' now that Gould does not 'convince' Conway Morris, at all. His book *The Crucible of Creation* was a direct response to Gould's theme of contingency and his subsequent book published two years after Gould's death *Life's Solution: Inevitable Humans in a Lonely Universe* was a continuation of Conway Morris theme of 'non-contingency'. See pp. 205 to 218 of *The Crucible of Creation.*

[42]Apart from the works by Conway Morris cited above see text and notes accompanying above note 37.

[43]Morris (n 12) 201, 206. See also text and notes accompanying above n 17, n 18 and n 19.

[44]According to Wikipedia article, Toynbee was born on 'April 14, 1889' and died on 'October 22, 1975'. Arnold J. Toynbee, https://en.wikipedia.org/wiki/Arnold_J._Toynbee.

[45]Cane (n 12). The blurb of the book states that the 'essays - written by experts in legal philosophy - do not re-run the Hart-Fuller debate, nor are they confined to discussion of the jurisprudential issues canvassed by Hart and Fuller. Rather, in using the debate as a point of departure and inspiration, they pick up on strands in the debate and re-evaluate them in the light of the social, political, and intellectual developments of the past 50 years, when the ways of understanding law and other normative systems have changed'. The original debate between the late Professor H.L.A Hart (1907–1992) and the late Professor Lon L. Fuller (1902–1978) was published in two *Harvard Law Review* articles namely HLA Hart 'Positivism and the Separation of Law and Morals' (1958) 71(4) *Harvard Law Review* 593–629 and Lon L Fuller, 'Positivism and Fidelty to Law - A Reply to Professor Hart' (1958) 71(4) *Harvard Law Review* 630–672.

[46]Whether Toynbee can, in addition to being a historian, be legitimately also described as a social scientist is irrelevant to exploring *a posterori* what Toynbee as a historian would have said on the Gould-Conway Morris debate on the nature of the development of natural history as embodied in their own views of evolution.

historian) would have said about a debate between two eminent scientists from what can be said to be the 'historical science'[47] of evolutionary theory and paleontology.

As far as Toynbee is concerned this writer would state that Toynbee is more of a 'teleologist' (though not in the mould of Augustine or Marx) than a 'contingent' historian regarding human history. Toynbee would probably eschewed Gould's view of 'contingency' as applied to – a few thousand years of human history – and may probably opt for teleology in human history as well. This of course is conjectural- and the reasons for this conjecture is elaborated below after the interlude from Ernst Mayr. In contrast, one of the twentieth century greatest evolutionists Ernst Mayr has (as stated and discussed below) stated that he has 'come to the conclusion that Gould is largely right'.

This writer would state that the historians of (recent) human history discussed in this Chapter (not extending more than several thousand years) that is Augustine of Hippo (in the fifth and fourth century of the Current Era), Karl Marx (in the nineteenth century), Arnold Toynbee (in the twentieth century) favours or adopts in their theologies and philosophies of history a form or various forms of teleology. The author believes that the discussions above and below indicate the 'positions' of these historians of human history and this author believes that the 'positions' they adopted are clear. This author also has inferred in the elaborations and arguments above and below that great as these personages (Augustine, Marx and Toynbee) were (and to use the historic present tense) this author (does *not* necessarily agree with their positions of what in a generic sense can be termed as 'teleology' of recent *human* history not extending much more than several thousand years. As far as the author of this Chapter is concerned in a few aspects of human history it is contingency rather than teleology which 'governs' it.

8.3.4 An Interlude on Ernst Mayr's Views on Contingency and Teleology

Deference to authority in 'hard' or physical sciences as well as in the historical and social sciences should not necessarily be a criteria – perhaps not even a 'factor' in gauging the validity of a scientific hypotheses. It is appropriate though to state that the late Ernst Mayr, considered as one of twentieth century's greatest evolutionists[48]

[47]The term 'historical science' is used by, among others, the late Ernst Mayr (1904–2005). See Ernst Mayr, *What Makes Biology Unique: Considerations on the Autonomy of a Scientific Discipline* (Cambridge University Press, 1st ed, 2007) where at page 32 Mayr states that 'Evolutionary Biology is a historical science'.

[48]See Carol Kesuk Yoon, 'Ernst Mayr, Pioneer in Tracing Geography's Role in the Origin of Species, Dies at 100', *New York Times* (5 February 2005). The very first sentence of the obituary states that 'Ernst Mayr, the leading evolutionary biologist of the twentieth century, died on Thursday in Bedford, Mass[achusetts]'. Coincidentally, the third paragraph of the obituary states that Ernst Mayr was 'known as an architect of the evolutionary or modern synthesis, an intellectual watershed when modern evolutionary biology was born. The synthesis, which was described by Dr. Stephen

had briefly commented on the essential argument of Gould (though not specifically on the Gould-Conway Morris debate) in one of his last books, first published in 2001,[49] when Mayr was 97 years old. Under a sub-heading 'Chance or Necessity' Mayr writes:

> … let us look at the 35 or so living phyla of animals. They are the survivors of the 60 or more body plans that existed in the early Cambrian…Many or most of their characteristics may have had their origin in a *developmental accident* that was tolerated by selection, while the seeming failure of those that became extinct may have been the result of a chance event (like the Alvarez asteroid extinction event). Gould (1989) made such contingencies a major theme in *Wonderful Life*, and *I have come to the conclusion that he is largely right.*[50]

Mayr does not make any reference to Simon Conway Morris post-1998 work[51] in his last two books published after 1998 namely *What Evolution Is* and *What Makes Biology Unique* first published in 2001 and 2004 respectively. Still, as early as 1974 Mayr has expressed his negative or at the very least skeptical views on a 'teleological interpretation' of evolution.[52] Conway Morris emphasizes on the importance of 'convergence' in his writings. More important, at least implicitly he has referred to his late father's view – which he endorsed – as being on the side of the angels.[53] In that sense and in this writer's opinion Conway Morris view has shades of teleology and perhaps at least in particular contexts they are informed by (Christian) theology.

Hence Ernst Mayr, if he were to 'take sides' in the Gould—Conway Morris debate, would arguably be not on the side of the 'angels'. Instead he would probably at least give a partial if not general endorsement of Gould's view over that of Conway Morris. This is based, as stated above, in a book published less than four years before his death Mayr has (in his own words) 'come to the conclusion that Gould 'is largely

---

Jay Gould of Harvard as "*one of the half-dozen major scientific achievements in our century,*" reconciled Darwin's theories of evolution with new findings in laboratory genetics and in fieldwork on animal populations and diversity'. (Emphasis added) New York Times, 5 February 2005.

[49]Ernst Mayr, *What Evolution Is* (Basic Books, 2001) 228. Emphases added.

[50]Ibid 229. One notes the 'authoritative' tone 'I have come to the conclusion …' of Mayr. If Conway Morris can designate Gould's thesis as 'trivial' and the authoritarian tone regarding his comments on Marxism and atheism Ernst Mayr's use of 'come to the conclusion' is not unjustified; in fact it is quite modest.

[51]As far as the debate between Gould and Conway Morris is concerned it could, for the purpose of this discussion be said to start in 1998 when Conway Morris published *The Crucible of Creation* and also an encapsulation of the debate was reproduced in *Nature* See text and note accompanying above note 15.

[52]See, eg, Ernst Mayr, 'Teleological and Teleonomic: A New Analysis' (1974) 14 *Boston Studies in the Philosophy of Science* 91–117.

[53]See text and notes accompanying above n 19. It is 'assumed' that Conway Morris does not believe in the actual, physical existence of 'angels' but (one hopes) in a counter-factual hypothetical if he does, one is tempted what evolutionary pathways and 'convergence' led to the existence of 'angels'. One realizes that Conway Morris was not being literal when he writes that his late father (and by implication) his views are on the side of the 'angels': that is correct, lofty, noble, and perhaps 'blessed by God' in a metaphorical sense. This writer is making his comments based on the metaphorical reading of Conway Morris' views.

right'.[54] In one of his last articles that Mayr published in the Journal *Science* at the age of 100, one of the leading doyens of twentieth century evolutionary biology and philosopher of biology states so unselfconsciously that 'evolutionary biology is an endless frontier and there is still plenty to be discovered. I only regret that I won't be present to enjoy these future developments'.[55] The series of Gifford Lectures by Conway Morris and 'culminating' in his piece 'Darwin was Right Up to a Point' where *ad hominem* attacks on atheism was made after the death of Mayr. Mayr may (or may not) find Conway Morris' Gifford lectures 'interesting' albeit unsurprising.[56] If Conway Morris' article in *The Guardian*[57] published on the 200th anniversary of Charles Darwin's birth[58] were to come to Mayr's attention (hypothetically) how would the great scientist respond to Conway Morris statement on Darwin being 'right up to a point'[59] and about his call to 'join' Conway Morris in celebrating beside the 'coffin of atheism' which would have 'few mourners'? In this regard, the following interchange between Mayr and his interviewer from *Skeptic* magazine that took place in the year 2000 is instructive:

> *Skeptic*: **You don't believe in God, but are you an agnostic or an atheist?**
>
> *Mayr*: I have the honesty to say I'm an atheist. There is nothing that supports the idea of a personal God. On the other hand, famous evolutionists such as Dobzhansky were firm believers in a personal God. He would work as a scientist all week and then on Sunday get down on his knees and pray to God.

---

[54]See text accompanying above n 50.

[55]Ernst Mayr, '80 Years of watching Evolutionary Scenery' (2004) 305(5680) *Science* 46, 47. This is the last sentence of Mayr's article which was published on 2 July 2004 – just a day before Mayr's 100th birthday.

[56]See text and notes accompanying above n 19.

[57]See text and notes accompanying above n 23.

[58]Ernst Mayr died on 3 February 2005 just nine days short of Darwin's 195th birthday (on 12 February 2005). Again in a counter-factual hypothetical if Mary were alive and were invited to write a short newspaper article on Darwin's bicentenary in 2009 would the 'Old Man of Evolutionary Theory espouse the same or even similar views as Conway Morris? Would have had 'crowed' – as some did see, eg, Richard Dawkins' *The God Illusion* (Bantam Books, 2006) that Darwinism synthesized and further developed in the twentieth century including by himself had dealt a final blow to 'theism' or to the 'God hypothesis'? Mayr's respectful tone at least in the *Skeptic* Interview of 2000 would indicate that he would eschew such triumphalism.

[59]As a non-specialist when one reads a claim written for non-specialists even though by a specialist, one has the right to express one's view and one would say that Conway Morriss claim that 'Darwin was right up to a point' is, taken the history of science, neither surprising nor is it that interesting. One can say that Copernicus was right up to a point (he proved that the Sun does not revolve around the Earth) and so was Newton whose 'rightness' up to a point was further complimented and expanded by other scientists including Albert Einstein in the fields of astrophysics, astronomy and cosmology. Mayr himself has written in many works about the initial incompleteness (*not invalidity*) of Darwin's theories but how it was refined and synthesized in the twentieth century. See among many others and eg 'The Maturation of Darwinism' in *What Makes Biology Unique* 117–132. In his continuing interest and the continuing discoveries in evolution theory see '80 Years of Watching Evolution Scenery' where he expressed his enthusiasm about the 'endless frontier of evolutionary biology' and his 'regret about him 'not being present to enjoy these developments' (text accompanying above note 60).

> *Skeptic*: What accounts for this style of thinking?
>
> *Mayr*: Frankly I've never been able to understand it because you would need two totally different compartments in your brain, one that deals with religion and the other with everything else.[60]

It is to be noted that Mayr did not make a blanket or *ad hominem* attack on theism or more specifically those who believe in a personal God. Compare that with Conway Morris' glib statements about the 'coffin of atheism' and 'its lack of mourners'. Instead, Mayr expressed puzzlement as to the reasons and not condescension to persons like Dobzhansky who were 'firm believers in a personal God'. One realizes though that on the other side of the (a)theistic divide there are persons like Richard Dawkins whose very strong criticism if not condemnations of perhaps most theistic beliefs *roughly* mirrors those of Conway Morris' attacks on atheism.[61]

At least in the excerpt from the interview in *Skeptic* the grand old man of twentieth century evolutionary theory was more modest, measured and indeed moderate in his pronouncements than either Dawkins is in his atheism or Conway Morris in his anti-atheism.

8.3.5 Toynbee on the Side of 'Teleology'?

After expressing the view that one of the twentieth centuries greatest evolutionists (Mayr) will side with Gould one would venture to guess what would have been Toynbee – one of twentieth century's greatest historians- views on the subject? With whose views Conway Morris or Gould, with which philosophical and historical perspective, Gould's 'contingency' or the Conway Morris view of 'convergence' would Toynbee be inclined to support? The answer seems fairly clear. Just as the grand old man of evolutionary theory of the twentieth century Mayr would opt for Gould's view the grand old historian of the twentieth century Toynbee would probably have been on the side of Conway Morris.

In trying to interpose Toynbee's views from *Time's* obituary on Toynbee on the Gould-Conway Morris debate a cross-discipline curiosity comes to mind. Toynbee traces the rise and fall of human civilizations in his life-time work. He apparently rejects Oswald Spengler's views on the rise and fall of human civilizations saying

[60] Michael Shermer and Frank J. Sulloway, 'The Grand Old Man of Evolution' (2000) 8 *Skeptic* 76, 82.

[61] This writer is not stating that certitudes displayed as seen in the title of Richard Dawkins' best seller *The God Delusion* and Conway Morris 'coffin of atheism' comment are rhetorical equivalents and therefore equally (in)valid or equally to be critiqued. For the record this writer has stated just as he believes that Ernst Mayr would, have sided more with Gould than with Simon Conway Morris in terms of 'contingency' and 'teleology' debate this writer is more with Dawkins than with Conway Morris in the differing if not very opposed views on religion and (a)theism of these two eminent scientists.

that 'civilization is not an organism. It is a product of wills'.[62] If 'civilization is a product of wills' was that the (collective) will of the peoples of the civilizations or was that in a 'higher sense' the will of God? One could add that – for the purpose of juxtaposing Toynbee's views on (human) history with the views mainly of Conway Morris on evolutionary history- the 'God' of Toynbee and the God of Conway Morris might not exactly be the same?[63] *Time* article elucidates that civilization being a product of wills, the wills or 'will' need not necessarily be that of humans only. For according to Toynbee (civilization) 'has a purpose. 'History', he wrote, [is] a vision of God's creation on the move'.[64] *Time* also stated that 'Toynbee was not committed to any religion. He involved himself deeply in Christianity and Buddhism but called himself an agonistic'.[65] This elaboration added a further dimension in discerning what Toynbee would have said to the contingency v convergence (or teleology) debate between an agnostic paleontologist[66] and a historian of science (Gould) and an Anglican paleontologist who has boldly declared the death of atheism (Conway Morris)?

---

[62]*Time*, 'Vision of God's Creation', November 3, 1975, n 1 '... while Spengler argued that the decay of civilizations was inexorable and essentially purposeless, Toynbee insisted that man retains his freedom of choice: "I do not believe that civilizations have to die ... Civilization is not an organism. It is a product of wills."'

[63]Even though Conway Morris' credentials as a palaeontologist qua palaeontologist is extremely impressive – though to this writer not necessarily his philosophy of natural history as is made obvious in his statements (n. 19) – Conway Morris would not have the same understanding of say, what was and is called the 'Eastern religions' as Toynbee did. Conway Morris could not appreciate to the same degree and level as Toynbee did the doctrines of, say for example, Buddhism. Moreover, though one cannot 'ground' one's claim with concrete quotes, Conway Morris, unlike Toynbee would not have stated and his recent writings indicate that he is not an 'agnostic'. Compare Ernst Mayr and Richard Dawkins' professed atheism, with that of Gould's respectful agnosticism as evinced from his NOMA (religion and science being Non-Overlapping Magisteria) that Gould proposed in his work first published in 1999 *Rocks of Ages: Science and Religion in the Fullness of Life* (Ballantine Books, 1999) and the 'agnosticism' of Toynbee and the increasingly theistic (if not creationist) views of Conway Morris.

[64]Ibid.

[65]Ibid. Compare this statement from *Time* magazine's book review of Toynbee's *A Study of History*: 'Toynbee also sees Christianity as the "climax of a continuous upward movement of spiritual progress" and thinks that "a twentieth century historian might venture to predict that Christianity's transfiguring effect on the World up to date would be outshone by its continuing operation in the future." But he does not accept Christianity as the only true religion. To do so, he believes, is a 'sin.' If to be a Christian is to believe that Christianity "possesses a monopoly of the Divine Light ... then I am not entitled to call myself a Christian." Since finishing the Study, Toynbee has expressed himself even more strongly. Said he: "If all the religions in the world were to disappear except Christianity and Buddhism, I would not be able to make a choice between them. In this part of the world, of course, it would be more convenient to keep Christianity, but convenience aside, there would be no choice between them for me."' See 'Books: Prophet of Hope and Fear' in October 18, 1954 issue of *Time* Magazine (reviewing Volumes VII to X of *A Study of History*).

[66]The term 'agnostic' is used to describe Gould's (non) religious views to the extent that I could discern from Gould's writings especially from his book *Rock of Ages*. Just as Conway Morris and Toynbee's invocation of 'Creation' in their philosophies of history can only be juxtaposed together: the 'agnosticisms' of Toynbee and Gould also can only be compared and not equated.

If (human) civilization is a product of wills, can we extrapolate, extend or interpose this metaphor to that of biological species?[67] One cannot say for sure whether or not Toynbee would consider the brevity, longevity and lastingness of (biological) species[68] to be a product of the 'wills of the species' a la human civilizations. But if as Toynbee states that (human) history is a 'vision of God's creation on the move', it would be logical to assume that regardless of whether it is human or natural history on Earth, history in the broad sense of the word is also 'God's creation on the move'.

Hence there seems to be more common ground or affinity between Conway Morris 'convergence' concept and Toynbee's view of history than between Gould's contingent history where the emergence of human intelligence – and consequently civilizations – is due to a concatenation of factors of extreme, staggering happenstances that, should the 'tape of life' be rerun, again (even a million times) humans would not emerge.

Hence the possible stand of Toynbee in support of Conway Morris is inferable though there could always be a 'counter factual' to this hypothetical analysis.

The purpose of this and above Sections is not to unequivocally state 'clearly' whether teleology is empirically, scientifically (as per 'hard sciences') correct – or not – as far as human history is concerned. It is to discuss such viewpoints. And as far as recent human history is concerned the writer has tried to espouse the teleology espoused by all three historians cum philosophers and comment on them. The fact that all three historians/philosophers espoused some form of 'teleology' did not (and does not) necessarily mean that they are 'objectively' (clearly?) correct. Also, this writer does not claim 'correctness' in his scepticism of teleology especially of both the Augustinian and Marxist 'brands'.

Juxtaposing human history of the past several thousand years and the attendant 'teleology'/'contingency' discourses or debates (if not in human history but then in

---

[67]Ernst Mayr's pioneering work *Systematics and the Origin of Species,* first published in 1942 did not make it to *Time* magazine's pages though Arnold Toynbee's publication, *A Study of History* was reviewed a few times. The publication of final volumes of *A Study of History* in 1954 was discussed in a feature length story in *Time.* See, 'Books: Prophet of Hope and Fear' above n 66.

[68]The dinosaurs for example 'lasted' around 160 million years and though the argument is not falsifiable (see for example' Bipedal Dinosaur as Alien' in Fig. 8 at page 197 in Michael Sheremer, *The Believing Brain: From Ghosts and Gods to Politics and Conspiracies – How We Construct Belief and Reinforce them as Truths* (Times Publication, 2011) and they could well have continued to exist but for the Alvarez asteroid. That at least was what Gould writes: '… dinosaurs … probably became extinct only as a quirky result of the most unpredictable of all events – a mass dying triggered by extra terrestrial impact. If dinosaurs had not died in this event, they would probably still dominate the domain of large body vertebrates, as they had for so long with such conspicuous success, and mammals would still be small creatures in the interstices of their world. The situation prevailed for a hundred million years why not for sixty million more? Since dinosaurs were not moving toward markedly larger brains, and since such a prospect may lie outside the capabilities of reptilian design, we must assume that consciousness could not have evolved on our planet if a cosmic catastrophe had not claimed the dinosaurs as victims. In an entirely literal sense, we owe our existence, as large and reasoning animals, to our lucky stars. Gould (n 9) 318. What would Toynbee had said to this claim? If 'civilizations' is a product of wills, does the fact of the dinosaurs' long lasting existence and reign on Earth a product of 'wills' or is that due of the product of God's inscrutable 'vision' or 'purpose'?

natural history pace the Gould-Conway Morris debate with a few statements by Mayr favouring, so to speak, contingency and Gould's view) may seem 'stretched'. To the best of this writer's knowledge they have not been attempted before. In order to try to 'push the boundaries of comparison' an attempt towards that end has been made in the first part of this Chapter.

Part Two: Toynbee's 'Intellectual Provincialism' and Spinoza's *Sub Specie Aeternitatis*

8.4 Intellectual Provincialism, 'Seeing as a Whole' and *Sub Species Aeternitatis*

The last segment of Toynbee's obituary in *Time* magazine states (by implication) Toynbee's view of the need to transcend 'intellectual provincialism' since 'the dogma that life is just one damn thing after another' does not fit in well with his 'lifetime conviction that human affairs do not become intelligible until they are seen as a whole.'[69]

The need to transcend so to speak the mundane affairs or travails of life as indicated by the phrase 'one damn thing after another' and the fact that human affairs becoming 'intelligible' only when they are 'seen as a whole' reminds this writer of a Latin phrase which supposedly originates from the seventeenth century philosopher Baruch Spinoza: *sub specie aeternitatis.*[70] Spinoza had been called a 'God intoxicated philosopher'[71] as well as that of a political[72] and ethical[73] philosopher. And at times both in a derogatory and condemnatory context Spinoza has been called an 'atheist'.[74] He has also, among others, considered as a proto-biologist who had

---

[69] *Time* (n 1).

[70] See, eg, Margaret Gullan-Whur, *Within Reason: A Life of Spinoza* (St. Martin's Press, 1998) 78 where the author explains the terms *sub specie aeternitatis* and *sub specie durationis. Time's* article of Monday, March 07, 1927 on the celebrations of the 250th death anniversary of Spinoza in Holland was entitled 'Education; Sub Specie Aeternitatis'. As a 'spill over' it can be analogized that more than 300 years after Spinoza apparently pioneered the use of the term *sub specie aeternitatis* the late Thomas Kuhn's use of the term 'paradigm shift' in *The Structure of Scientific Revolutions* (University of Chicago Press, 1962) popularised it. Perhaps Kuhn's 'paradigm shift' is used more among the scientists including the social scientists whereas the phrase *sub specie aeternitatis* would mainly be limited to philosophers.

[71] See, eg, 'Sub Specie Aeternitatis', n1 where Spinoza was stated to have been 'indifferent to whether men called him 'this famous atheist' or 'the God intoxicated man'. See also for a twentieth century biography Lewis Browne, *Spinoza, God-Intoxicated Man: Three Books Which Marks the Three Hundredth Anniversary of the Philosopher's Birth Blessed Spinoza, A Biography* (Macmillan Company, 1932).

[72] The title of the only book dealing with philosophy published in his life time was entitled *Tractatus Theologico Politiicus (Theologico-Political Treatise).*

[73] Spinoza's main work published posthumously was entitled *Ethica: Ordine Geometrico Demonftrata* (*Ethics: Demonstrated in Geometrical Order*).

[74] For a negative or condemnatory use of the word 'atheist' see *Time's* 1927 article, *Sub Specie Aeternatis* beliefs' (n 71). See also Steven Nadler, *Spinoza: A Life* (Cambridge University Press, 1999).

uncanny insights to modern day neurology.[75] Spinoza was not a historian in the mould of a Toynbee who was born more than two hundred and fifty years after him[76] nor that of say, Herodotus, 'the father of history' born about 2100 years before Spinoza.[77] Hence this excursion into Spinoza's philosophy is not to extend the contingency v convergence debate by speculating as to what Spinoza would have said on these issues. Rather this commentary is an attempt to explore whether a comparison or not can be made between the phrase *sub specie aeternitatis* of Spinoza with what can be said to be Toynbee's philosophy of life[78] which asserts that 'human affairs do not become intelligible until they are seen as a whole'.[79]

If *sub specie aeternitatis* essentially means 'an honorific expression which is universally and eternally true without any reference to or dependence upon the merely temporal portions of reality'[80] then perhaps it does not fully equate with Toynbee's statement of human affairs being 'intelligible' only 'when they are seen as a whole'. Toynbee as such does not (perhaps) (necessarily) states that his view(s) of history is 'universally true'. Spinoza's *sub specie durationis* means that it is 'conceived … under an aspect of time and place [and] is [therefore] inadequate'.[81] Spinoza's 'fond[ness] of viewing things *sub specie aeternitatis* (from the view point of eternity)'[82] and Toynbee's 'life-time conviction' and indeed by implication his advise to 'see things as a whole' in order to make human affairs 'intelligible' overcoming as it were the 'intellectual provincialism' of the 'dogma that life is one damned thing after another' can be juxtaposed and studied. The two sages of the 17th and twentieth centuries[83] were putting forth their exhortations that one should to try to escape

But compare another biographer of Spinoza Margaret Gullan-Whur's contention 'while Spinoza did not acknowledge a theistic God (that is supernatural, and enjoying a personal relationship with his Creatures) the question of whether he was an atheist in the commonly accepted sense is still open to debate, for *God, or Nature* really existed for Spinoza …God did not exist just philosophically, but was all there is *existentially* speaking' (emphases in original). *Within Reason* (n 74) 91.

[75] See generally, Antonio Damasio, *Looking for Spinoza: Joy, Sorrow and the Feeling Brain* (Mariner Books, 2003).

[76] According to *Wikipedia* Spinoza was born on November 24, 1632 and died on February 21, 1677. 'Baruch Spinoza', http://en.wikipedia.org/wiki/Spinoza (accessed 17 July 2011) and Arnold J. Toynbee was born on April 14, 1889 and died on October 22, 1975 http://en.wikipedia.org/wiki/Arnold_J._Toynbee (17 July 2011).

[77] According to *Wikipedia* Herodotus lived in the fifth century BC (circa 483-425) BC. https://en.wikipedia.org/wiki/Herodotus.

[78] Toynbee's obituary in *Time* states about Toynbee's 'life time conviction' about human affairs only being intelligible only when they are seen as a whole and this can in a generic sense be considered the historian's philosophy of life.

[79] See *Time* (n 1).

[80] See text and notes accompanying above n 71.

[81] *Within Reason* (n 71) 78.

[82] *Time* (n 71). *Time's* article of 1927 states that Spinoza was 'fond of saying he viewed things *sub specie aetenitatis*'.

[83] Spinoza's twentieth century biographer Margaret Gullan-Whur perhaps with a touch of irony mentioned that Spinoza during the time he spent in the Dutch town of Rijnsburg was its 'sage'. *Within Reason* (n 71) 117. The last sub-title of Toynbee's obituary in *Time* (Education: Vision of

from the snares of provincialism[84] of theirs (and our own) times and space(s), the tyranny of the here and now, to see things in perspective and to a certain extent with detachment. Apparently, these sages have managed to overcome the provincialisms of their times and places to a certain extent and this apparently was achieved by Spinoza through his philosophizing[85] and Toynbee by his historic or at least land mark 'writings on the broad sweep of history'.[86]

Sub Specie Aeternitatis *and 'Eternity' in Emily Dickinson's Poem*

Two centuries after Spinoza, Emily Dickinson[87] in her poem 'Because I Could Not Stop for Death' uses the phrase 'eternity' as the last word of the last sentence in the last stanza of the poem. The poem reads:

> Because I could not stop for Death,
> He kindly stopped for me;
> The carriage held but just ourselves
> And Immortality.
> We slowly drove, he knew no haste,
> And I had put away
> My labor, and my leisure too,
> For his civility.
> We passed the school, where children strove
> At recess, in the ring;
> We passed the fields of gazing grain,
> We passed the setting sun.
> Or rather, he passed us;
> The dews grew quivering and chill,

God's Creation (n 1)) is 'international sage': 'He had become an international sage, like Einstein, Schweitzer or Bertrand Russell, who was asked for his opinion on all manner of subjects'.

[84]The late Daniel Boorstin who in late 1975 was 'confirmed as the new Librarian of Congress' stated that Toynbee was one of very 'few historians [who] have spent themselves so unstintingly or so effectively in the effort to transcend the provincialism of their time and place *Time* (n 1).

[85]*Time's* article of 1927 ('Sub Specie Aeternitatis' reports that in February 1927 on the 250th anniversary of Spinoza's death '[a]n international congress sat to philosophize in his name'. One wonders when the 250th anniversary of Toynbee's death takes place in the twenty-third century (that would be the year 2225) whether an 'international congress would sat to philosophize' about Toynbee's philosophy of history! As regards the qualification that Spinoza was only to a certain extent successful in 'overcoming the provincialism' of *his* time and place notwithstanding his 'fondness' to look things *sub specie aeternitatis* can be seen, claims one of his biographer, in Spinoza's attitudes towards women. Margaret Gullan-Whur (*Within Reason* (n 71) 186, see also (295–98) claims that Spinoza's views on women belongs merely in the category of *sub species durationis*.

[86]*Time's* obituary of Toynbee quoted 'Harvard's Samuel Eliot Morison' as saying that Toynbee was 'one of the few people who dared to write on the broad sweep of history' ('Vision of God's Creation).

[87]'Emily Dickinson' Wikipedia states that Dickson was born December 10, 1830 and died on May 15, 1886. https://en.wikipedia.org/wiki/Emily_Dickinson.

For only gossamer my gown,
My tippet only tulle.
We paused before a house that seemed
A swelling of the ground;
The roof was scarcely visible,
The cornice but a mound.
Since then 'tis centuries, and yet each
Feels shorter than the day
I first surmised the horses' heads
Were toward eternity.[88]

Needless to say Dickinson was familiar with =perhaps even immersed in – Christian thought though she could not be said to be a 'Christian poet' say, to the same degree as the Anglican English poet George Herbert.[89] One does not know whether or not Dickinson was familiar with the works of Spinoza and his use of the term '*sub specie aeternitatis*'. One could surmise that her use of the word 'eternity' might be considered as 'neo-Christian' and might or might not have Christian theological implications.

The term 'eternity' used by Spinoza and Dickinson might (or might not) have differing connotations. Spinoza's concept of 'eternity' could have less Christian theological connotations than Dickson's philosophy and metaphysics which is discernible, deductible or interpretable from the above poem. On a spectrum of metaphysical or theological connotations whose concept is the most Christian or neo-Christian: the ethical and moral philosophy of Spinoza, the 'eternity' to which the 'horse's head are turned' as stated in the poem of Dickinson, the 'vision of God's creation' of Toynbee, and the discernible theological connotations of aspects of Simon Conway's evolutionary postulates? Whose views – Dickinson, Toynbee and Conway Morris – would Spinoza have considered closest to his viewing 'things' *sub specie aeternitatis*?

Even though there are similarities as has been argued between Spinoza's viewing things under 'an aspect of eternity' and also Toynbee's seeing 'human affairs becoming intelligible only when they are viewed as a whole' Spinoza's *weltanschauung* may even be more ambitious than Toynbee. For Toynbee was specific that the intellectual transcendence (since the 'intellectual provincialism' is to be overcome or be transcended) which he recommends is regards human affairs only. In contrast by using the term 'eternity' Spinoza appears to have a broader sweep in his claimed perspective at looking at 'things'.

Spinoza as well as Emily Dickinson had used the word 'eternity' in their writings two centuries apart. Due to the historical fact of the 'provincialisms of their times and places' (though no fault of their own) they were not privy to the scientific knowledge

[88] There are numerous versions of the poem on the world wide web. This version was taken from http://academic.brooklyn.cuny.edu/english/melani/cs6/stop.html (17 July 2011).

[89] See, eg, James Boyd White, *This Book of Starres: Learning to Read George Herbert* (University of Michigan Press, 1995).

of how old the Universe (in the astronomical sense) is.[90] Neither could they have envisaged the age of the Earth and the immensity, from a temporal human perspective, of geological time or the history of life involving as it does those of the existence and extinctions of billions of species on Earth in the 3800 million history of life on Earth.[91] Such a biological overlay to that of geological time needs to be made not only because the perspective of Toynbee-though not that of Spinoza- on the evolutionary issues and the nature of (non-human) history and emergence of human species has been discussed. Such an overlay of geological time and biological diversity is also called for in order to encompass the idea of eternity in its Earth bound temporal sense the existence of non-human species.

It is true that in the (strict) Spinozist sense of the word – at least according to one definition generally accepted – 'eternity' does not merely or mainly mean looking at things from the vastness of astronomical, geological and biological time or in the time frame of the emergence of life on Earth. Instead, it comprises the claim about 'universal[] and eternal tru[ths] without any reference to or dependence upon the merely temporal portions of reality'.[92] Still, at least in the generally understood sense of the word 'from the view point of eternity' as used in *Time's* magazine's 1927 article means 'view[ing] things … from the perspective of eternity'.[93] This general notion would or should entail such a broad perspective including in the 'time-bound' sense of the word the immensity of astronomical and geological time. It could be quibbled that 'time' and 'eternity' are two different contexts and the response would be that one need not be that fastidious in making sense and sensibility (with reference to the title of Jane Austen's novel) of the need to have a broad or 'eternal' perspective as indicated in the life philosophies of Spinoza and Toynbee.

If it is granted, for the purpose of this discussion, that 'eternity' includes the broad reaches of space and time (space-time) then even taken into account Earth's geological time, and compared with say, the existence and extinction of the Dinosaurs is an insignificant event in the perspective of the Universe which has lasted about 13.6 billion years with hundreds of millions (if not billions) of galaxies and billions of stars whereas Dinosaurs dominated the Earth an extremely small corner of the Universe for a mere 160 million years. Like wise, if one carries viewing things from an 'aspect of eternity' vis-à-vis for example the Holocaust and many other genocides of the twentieth and previous centuries[94] they might from the 'perspective of eternity' as a negligible 'blips'.

---

[90] See generally Stephen Hawking, *A Brief History of Time* (Bantam Books, 1988). For an inadequate response to Hawking's immensely popular book see, Roy E Peacock, *A Brief History of Eternity, A Considered Response to Stephen Hawking's A Brief History of Time* (Crossway Books, 1990). See also Hawking and Blodinow (n 2).

[91] As to the immensity of geological time, see, eg, Stephen Jay Gould, *Time's Arrow, Time's Cycle: Myth and Metaphor in the Discovery of Geological Time(Jerusalem Harvard Lectures)* (Harvard University Press, 1988).

[92] See text above n 71.

[93] See above n 71. *Time* Magazine' Sub Specie Aeternitatis'.

[94] See, eg, Adam Jones, *Genocide: A Comprehensive Introduction* (Routledge, 2010).

Based on these grand astronomical and geological time (and perhaps 'eternity') 'a Devil's Advocate' view as to the two sages' (Spinoza's and Toynbee's) exhortation to overcome provincialism of temporal times and places can be made. Such a 'Devil's Advocate' view would run along these lines: If the Holocaust and the genocides that occurred in human history is considered from the viewpoint of eternity then a possible interpretation, 'stretched' may be somewhat distorted is perhaps but not necessarily *reduction ad absurdum* claim that could arise is that these tragedies, 'man's inhumanities to man' and can be 'intelligible' albeit only in the broad scheme of things from a human (history) perspective they are 'negligible blips' viewed 'as a whole'. Speaking purely from that standpoint then at times a narrower outlook which does not always and necessarily discounts or 'shelves' the provincialism of the times and places might perhaps need to be adopted.

Regarding the above paragraphs the reviewer of the chapter states:

> that '[i]n between citations from Spinozean notion of eternity and terming genocides as negligible 'blips' defeat the whole purpose of the essay.

The writer of this chapter has specifically stated above (twice) that his use of the word 'blips' and attendant implication *was 'a Devil's Advocate view'* (with D and A in caps). It is repeated here that this writer does not (does not) endorse from the viewpoint of *sub specie durationis* or for that matter *sub specie aeternitatis* that the genocides which did occur in human history are in retrospect not regrettable or they are to be remain unacknowledged. These mass killings (to use the more vernacular rather than the at times more legalistic 'genocide') did occur even before the times of the earliest historians namely Augustine discussed briefly and Herodotus (only) mentioned above. The writer did not –does not- state that these are not to be (at least from the perspective of the present) to be 'ignored' or are 'unimportant'. But they did occur.[95] The writer also realises that *sub specie aetenatitis* (looking from the aspect of eternity perhaps does not necessarily mean astronomical, geological time as explained above but (again) in a stretched manner the writer wrote 'blips' with the caveat that it is a 'Devil's Advocate' point of view. Perhaps the criminality as an international law offence of stemming from the adoption and coming into force of the *1948 Convention on the Prevention and Punishment of the Crime of Genocide* arguably from the aspect of duration (*sub specie durationis*) occurred not that long ago: the year 1951 when the *Genocide Convention* came into force.

As for allegedly 'defeating' the 'whole purpose of the essay' the writer has stated at the start of this Chapter what are the contents or the issues to be covered and by implication what was (and is) 'the whole purpose of the essay'. Perhaps the 'purpose of this second Part is to compare and contrast Toynbee's eschewing of 'intellectual provincialism' with Spinoza's exhortation to view (to borrow from *Time*'s obituary of

[95]When the writer uses the term 'genocide' he does not mean the 'legalistic' meaning of genocide (in international law comprising international criminal, humanitarian and human rights law) under the *1948 Convention on the Prevention and Crime of Genocide* where, among others, the 'crime of genocide' with caveats and elaborations, qualifications, is binding and 'punishable' only after the *Genocide Convention* came into force.: that is the year 1951. When the writer writes 'genocide' he does not mean in the legalistic sense but in the general sense of the word.

Toynbee) 'human affairs' from aspects of eternity. If the *whole* purpose of the *entire* essay is to provide a traditional and generally positive view of Spinoza's laudable or at least in the largely positive sense of the words of (always?) looking at things (from the viewpoint of eternity) then it might arguably 'defeat the whole point' of (even then the writer would claim at most) Part II of the essay. But the second part of the essay (and only a few parts of Part II of this Chapter) is to compare Spinoza's notion of looking things from the perspective of eternity and Toynbee's life-time or life-long belief that to make human affairs intelligible it is necessary to view things as a whole.

8.5 Design, Consilience, Emergence and Spinozist View Points

8.5.1 Design/Intelligent Design v Spinozist Notions

This sub-section is inserted after the reviewer's comments that this section 'needs to critique Spinozean [sic for Spinozist} and theistic viewpoints from the contemporary debate between Design, Consilience and Emergence if any proper position to be obtained'.

The reviewer has used the word 'position' twice and in the above comment the reviewer qualifies it as (a) 'proper position'. This writer submits that in discussing metaphysical topics and even general philosophical topics it is not always necessary or mandatory to adopt or perhaps even discern far less determine conclusively and unequivocally what the 'proper' position is or was. This would be so even in partly legal, partly moral, partly philosophical topics such as that between the Hart-Devlin debate on the enforcement of morals by legislation as discussed in the Chapter by Choong Jung Min.[96] In the Chapter Choong Jun Min opts, in general, the position of Devlin to that of Hart but is that a proper position or not?

Still, party addressing the reviewer's concern over proper positions the author will try to address (albeit) briefly:

8.5.2 Design, Intelligent Design v Deus Sive Natura

Over 200 years after the death of Spinoza, William Paley (July 1743–25 May 1805) in the year 1802 published Natural *Theory*[97] where he postulated, indeed asserted that

[96]Choong Jun Min 'Relevance of Hart-Devlin Debate on Recent International Law Developments Especially in Relation to the International Criminal Court', Chapter VII, this Volume.

[97]William Paley, *Natural Theory or Evidence of the Existence and Attributes of the Deity, Collected from the Experiences of Nature* (Oxford University Press, 1802). A more recent edition was published in 2008 (edited by Matthew D. Eddy) as an Oxford World Classic.

claims that the natural world and humans have emerged out of nothing is tantamount to claiming that a watch came into existence without a watch maker: therefore there is (was) a Creator who not only created the world but brings all sentient beings (to use a largely Buddhist term) into existence. Paley of course published his tract 52 years before Charles Darwin's *Origin of Species.*[98]

One does not know whether or not Paley was familiar with Spinoza's mainly posthumously published philosophical works especially the *Ethics*[99] but even if he does one supposes that Paley would not accept or embrace Spinoza's pantheism or the concept of *Dues Sives Natura* ('God or Nature'). Would Spinoza have agreed with or approved of Paley's 'Blind Watchmaker"[100] thesis? Spinoza in his posthumously published *Ethics* tried to prove his thesis with 'geometrical' methods. Would Spinoza be impressed by Paley's watch-maker 'proof' of the existence of the (Christian) Deity? Perhaps not. Regardless of Paley's proof the God of Spinoza was not (arguably) a personal Deity outside of nature which created (creates) the World like a watch maker making the watch outside of the watch, so to speak. Perhaps being (more than a little?) mischievous this writer can postulate that according to Spinoza both the watch-maker and the watch are the same.

It might be stated that the issues raised by William Paley is 'old'. The contemporary debate regarding 'intelligent design' can only be briefly touched upon.

The phrase 'intelligent design' in the contemporary period was first arguably and (designedly) used in a book *Of Pandas and People*[101] in 1989 when two years earlier the United States Supreme Court held in the case of *Edwards v Aguillard* that the state of Louisiana's 'Balanced Treatment Act' which stated that where evolution science is taught in the Louisiana's public schools then 'creation science' must also be taught is unconstitutional. The United States Supreme Court held by a vote of seven to two that the Louisiana Act to be unconstitutional.[102] After the teaching of creation science was held unconstitutional the phrase 'creation science' was eschewed to be replaced by the phrase 'intelligent design' as it was stated in the case of *Kitzmiller v. Dover Area School District*[103] in the United States District Court for the Middle District of Pennsylvania. In that case it was observed by Judge John E Jones II that in two successive 1987 drafts of the book, over one hundred uses of the root word 'creation', such as 'creationism' and "Creation Science", were changed to "intelligent design"[104] Specifically in the field of evolutionary biology Michael Behe in his *Darwin's Black*

---

[98] *On the Origin of Species by Means of Natural Selection, or the Preservation of Favoured Races in the Struggle for Life* (First edition) (John Murray, 1859).

[99] The first edition *Ethica, ordinegeometricodemonstrata* (published in Latin) 'Ethics Demonstrated in Geometrical Order' was published posthumously in 1677 the same year Spinoza died. A recent English translation is Benedict de Spinoza, *The Ethics*, tr RHM Elwes (Wilder Publications, 2007).

[100] Reference is made to Richard Dawkins, *The Blind Watchmaker: Why the Evidence of Evolution Reveals a Universe without Design* (Norton and Company, 1986).

[101] Percival Davis and Dean H Kenyon, *Of Pandas and People*, Charles Thaxton (ed) (Foundation for Thoughts and Ethics, 1989).

[102] *Edwards v Aguillard*, 482 US 578 (1987).

[103] 400 F Supp 2d 707.

[104] Ibid 31–37 *par tim.*

Box[105] also propounded his views of 'Intelligent Design' as applied to (evolutionary) biology.

To briefly address the reviewer's comments as regards Spinozist and theistic viewpoints the author will state that:

(1) Spinozist and theistic viewpoints are arguably mutually exclusive since Spinoza's 'theism'[106] if it was *that* could not be designated as Christian theism. In contrast the (indirect theism if not creationism) of most intelligent designers (in the United States) is not only theism but also Christian theism.

(2) To label Spinoza's philosophical views his would have to be designated as 'pantheism' rather than 'theism'.

(3) It is somewhat anomalous indeed almost self-contradictory to critique at least from the view points of 'intelligent design' (as mainly though *not* exclusively originated from and espoused in the United States) 'theism' for most,- at the very least some- of the intelligent designers would espouse theism if not (Christian) creationism.[107]

(4) What would most of the intelligent designers comment on *Sives Du Nature* of Spinoza? Most of the current intelligent designers for want of better words would have put the intelligent designer outside of Nature and therefore Spinoza's 'equation' of God and Nature would for them be at the very least anomalous and at worst if not heretical then invalid and wrong.

(5) What would Spinoza have thought of 'intelligent design' arguments? The metaphysician, moral, political, ethical philosopher and proto-biologist Spinoza of the seventeenth century would have to learn among others Darwin's evolutionism, creationism and 'intelligent designism' so to speak for him to comment on intelligent design. It would have been a guess (by the author) that Spinoza's 'proofs' of his ethical postulates through geometrical methods might (or) might not have affinities with the method(s) and claims of the intelligent designers. Predominantly though to the extent that the intelligent designers put their 'Designer' (or Creator) arguably outside of Nature, the gentle philosopher of the seventeenth century might well have remained unconvinced by the designs of the late 20th and early twenty-first century intelligent designers.

8.5.3 *Consilience (Perhaps) Could Be in Spinoza's Mind*

The word 'consilience' was apparently first devised by William Whewell (1794–1861) roughly meaning (among others) 'unity of knowledge' where as used by Whewell 'the consilience of inductions' as in 'jumping together of knowledge'. In the words of Whewell:

---

[105] Michael Behe, *Darwin's Black Box: The Biochemical Challenge to Evolution* (Free Press, 1996).

[106] For an argument that Spinoza was not quite (even) a pantheist but an atheist see comments of Steven Nadler n 74.

[107] See, e.g., 'Christ is indispensable to any scientific theory, even if its practitioners don't have a clue about him. The pragmatics of a scientific theory can, to be sure, be pursued without recourse to Christ. But the conceptual soundness of the theory can in the end only be located in Christ'. William A Dembski, *Intelligent Design: The Bridge Between Science and Theology* (Intervarsity Press, 1999). Compare another intelligent designer Philip E. Johnson calling intelligent design proponents to hide their religious motivations so as to avoid having intelligent design identified 'as just another way of packaging the Christian evangelical message.' Philip E Johnson, 'Keep the Darwinists Honest', *Citizen* (April 1999).

> The Consilience of Inductions takes place when an Induction, obtained from one class of facts, coincides with an Induction obtained from another different class. Thus Consilience is a test of the truth of the Theory in which it occurs.[108]

More than 150 years after the first publication of Whewell's book the Harvard scientist, socio biologist Edward Wilson published his book, in 1998, *Consilience: The Unity of Knowledge.*[109] There is a single mention of Spinoza in Wilson's book. It reads:

Baruch Spinoza, the preeminent Jewish philosopher of the seventeenth century, visualized the deity as a transcendent substance present everywhere in the universe. *Deus sivenatura,* God or nature, he declared, they are interchangeable.[110]

This is only an 'executive summary' of Spinoza's metaphysics or philosophy but from the arguments put forth in the particular paragraphs Spinoza was mentioned by Wilson in the context of 'depersonalising' (the Creator) so to speak in aspects of Western thought. There is no specific critique by Edward O. Wilson, the modern espouser of 'Consilience' of Spinoza's concept of *Dues sivenatura* though in a later interview Wilson did state that 'he is not an atheist but a scientist and even an agnostic'.[111] To the extent that Spinoza was generally designated as pantheist (rather than an agnostic) it may be that the views of the twentieth and early twenty-first century evolutionist, sociobiologist Edward O. Wilson and seventeenth century philosopher Spinoza, who was among others termed a 'proto-biologist' may not be identical. This writer has read the description of Spinoza as pantheist, 'God-intoxicated philosopher' and 'atheist' in both the negative and complimentary sense of the word but not as 'agnostic'.

Since the 'unity of all things' an idea reflected in modern (in the mid-nineteenth century) and contemporary eras in the late twentieth century to early twenty-first century mainly as espoused by Edward O. Wilson[112] can arguably be also discerned if only inchoately in Spinoza's monist philosophy this writer ventures to suggest that unlike the designedly religiously purposive and purported 'Intelligent Design' idea Spinoza might arguably agree with and endorse the concept of Consilience.

Emergence v Spinoza's Determinism: Compatible or Not?

The referee's final comment was that this writer should also 'critique Spinozean viewpoints from the contemporary debate between Design, Consilience and Emergence if any proper position has [sic for is] to be obtained'. In the above sections the

---

[108] William Whewell, *The Philosophy of the Inductive Sciences, Founded Upon Their History* (John W Parker, 1840).

[109] Edward O Wilson, *Consilience: The Unity of Knowledge* (Vintage Press, 1999).

[110] Ibid 287.

[111] Penny Sarchet, 'Why Do We Ignore Warning about Earth's Future', *Slate* (1 February 2015) https://slate.com/technology/2015/02/e-o-wilson-on-the-meaning-of-human-existence-warnings-about-earths-future-and-religious-faith.html.

[112] Apart from Edward O. Wilson's seminal book *Consilience* see also a Springer Link publication Darren Delcher, *Consilience for Universal Design: the Emergence of a Third Culture* (Springer 2006).

writer has attempted to discern albeit in the context of the paper and the word limit assigned to it briefly and cursorily. This final sub-section will attempt to juxtapose another aspect of Spinoza's philosophy: his determinism.

There is Springer Link book which discusses in detail *Consilience, Truth and the Mind of God*[113] where in two Chapters 'Abiogenesis: The Emergence of Life from Non-Living Matter' (Chap. 5),[114] and 'Paleopsychology: The Emergence of Mind in the Universe' (Chap. 6)[115] is discussed. Another synonymous – not identical – term for Emergence is 'fine-tuning'.[116]In effect the 'Emergence' or 'Fine Tuning' arguments assert that in the physical Universe if several fundamental constants were only slightly different, the Universe would be unlikely to be conducive to the establishment and development of matter, astronomical structures, elemental diversity, or life as it is understood.[117] Hence if 'things' were a little different, so to speak not only human beings would *not* arise, galaxies would not be formed, the solar system might not come into existence and the Earth might not be formed. The author's humble view is that 'emergence' or 'fine tunings' argument has (in addition to its – almost – obvious theistic connotations) arguably can be seen from the (philosophical-scientific) perspective of determinism so that despite such odds, galaxies, solar systems, including this particular ('our') solar system, Earth and humans did arise so they are destined, philosophically and scientifically determined to arise, so to speak.

On the other hand an obverse argument can be made for – to revert to a word which has hitherto been absent in this section – the thesis of 'contingency'. Physicist Paul Davies suggested if the strong nuclear force were 2% stronger then it could drastically alter the physics of stars and all of the [this] Universe hydrogen would be consumed after the first few minutes [sic][118] of the Big Bang.[119] Fast forward, so to speak, about 13 billion (minus or plus a few hundred million years) to a place called Earth roughly between 525 and 430 million years ago. Stephen Jay Gould made the argument that if *Pikaia* has not survived the Burgess Shale decimation then we (that is humans and mammals) would not be here (on Earth).[120] The author ponders whether the issue of emergence/fine tuning (mainly though not entirely made

---

[113]Richard JD Rocco, *Consilience, Truth and the Mind of God[:] Science, Philosophy and Theology in the Search for Ultimate Meaning* (Springer Link 2018, corrected publication 2019).

[114]Ibid 69–80.

[115]Ibid 81–105.

[116]For only one among many others which deal with the concept of fine-tuning see Martin Rees, *Just Six Numbers the Deep Forces that Shape the Universe* (Basic Books, 2001).

[117]Ibid Martin Rees *par tim*. See also Paul Davies, *Cosmic Jackpot: Why Our Universe is Just Right for Life* (Penguin, 2007). But compare (or perhaps *contra*) Marcus Chown, 'Why the Universe wasn't fine-tuned for Life' (2011) 2816 *New Scientist* 5–65.

[118]Perhaps at the 'time' of the Big Bang albeit not immediately 'after' it 'time' – a human construct, so to speak – did not (does not) exist Still it is human terms and human 'time' that has to be used. See, eg, Steven Weinberg, *The First Three Minutes* (Basic Books, 1977).

[119]Paul Davies, *The Accidental Universe* (Cambridge University Press, 1993) 70–71. But contra J McDonald, D J Mullan 'Big Bang Nucleo Synthesis: the Strong Nuclear Force Meets the Weak Anthropic Principle' (2009) 80 (4) *Physical Review.*

[120]See Gould (n 8)321–34 as reproduced in n 15.

in the context of cosmology) when applied to evolution (non-humans or humans) can display (depending on how one takes it) of purpose, design or on the other hand contingency and a term specifically used by Paul Davies in his 1993 book (*The Accidental Universe*) accident, chance or even 'luck'.[121] Additionally and stretching the argument somewhat issues concerning determinism, non-determinism, randomness or contingency can be extrapolated on the 'emergence' and/or 'fine-tuning' issue. And that brings Spinoza, one more time, into this discussion.

In addition to being (an) arguable pantheist as far as his metaphysics is concerned Spinoza can perhaps be also be termed as a philosophical determinist. In the previous sub-sections in juxtaposing the intelligence design 'thesis' and the (arguably) less religiously motivated consilience issue the focus point in this writer's brief extrapolations is to the Spinoza's *deus sive nature* concept. Here the author will mainly focus on Spinoza's philosophical determinism and try to tie or delink, as the case may be, to the *possible* issue of determinism or accident, chance or contingency that can be discerned from the concepts arising from 'emergence' and 'fine-tuning'.

As far as human free will is concerned it may be safe to presume that Spinoza was a philosophical determinist. The following is a quote from the extant correspondence of Spinoza:

> Further conceive, I beg, that a stone, while continuing in motion, should be capable of thinking and knowing, that it is endeavoring, as far as it can, to continue to move. Such a stone, being conscious merely of its own endeavor and not at all indifferent, would believe itself to be completely free, and would think that it continued in motion solely because of its own wish. This is that human freedom, which all boast that they possess, and which consists solely in the fact, that men are conscious of their own desire, but are ignorant of the causes whereby that desire has been determined.[122]

It is realized that Spinoza was writing about free will v determinism of humans and the 'emergence' or 'fine-tuning' issue goes back so to speak cosmologically even as far as the 'Big Bang' and to cascade further many billions of years. From the Big Bang 'moving forward' billions of years to the contingency or emergence issue regarding the pathways of evolution as discerned above in the Gould-Morris debate. With respect, Spinoza would not be privy to these scientific and philosophical issues and in a sense this writer also finds it hard if not to critique or even comment on 'Spinozist and theistic viewpoints' or indeed to extrapolate, modify or 'innovate' Spinozist viewpoints without indulging in guess work and 'whimsy'.

The above excerpt of the stone example of Spinoza where a lifeless stone is devised as a 'live' human person as an allegory has been used on a very different philosophical topic. In Plato's *Crito* in the middle or 'midst' of a conversation between Socrates and his friend Crito. 'The Laws' of Athens came 'alive' and spoke to Socrates.[123] *The*

---

[121] Not only in cosmology and evolution references to luck can also be discerned in legal discourse. See Note, 'The Luck of the Law: Allusions to Fortuity in Legal Discourse' (1989) 102(8) *Harvard Law Review* 1862–1882.

[122] Spinoza, Letter to G.H, Schaller (October 1674) as cited in Peter D Mathews, 'Spinoza's Stone; The Logic of Donnie Darko' (2005) 25(1) *Post Script: Essays in Film and the Humanities* 38.

[123] Plato, *Crito*, tr Benjamin Jowett (Create Space Independent Publishing, 2015) 5, 15–21.

Laws if not scolded then at least chided Socrates of any idea of escaping from prison and at least indirectly 'disabused' Socrates friend Crito for harboring such intentions – that is helping Socrates to escape from prison. One does not know whether or not Spinoza had read the *Crito* in Dutch, Hebrew or Latin translations in the mid-seventeenth century. Spinoza's stone analogy though is arguably less-well known than Plato's literary device of 'The Laws' coming alive and speaking to Socrates.

In Spinoza's stone example the stone were to come alive – though Spinoza did not use the word or at least it was not discernible in the translation it would have thought it had 'free will'. The writer would admittedly with hesitation and (again) admittedly in a stretched manner puts forth this 'scenario': let's assume that the (now) conscious stone knew it was 'flying' in the air but for a relatively very long time did not develop consciousness or thought. In the latter stages of its flight the stone came to be aware that it is indeed surprising that it was (or is) travelling (in the air) thus and might began to ponder what about the causes that he was travelling. Was it an invisible hand that threw it? What concatenation of circumstances, events, emergence or 'fine tuning' brought about its 'flight'?

Let's replace 'stone' with a cannon ball to 'allow' a longer time-frame for the purpose of juxtaposing Spinoza's stone example with the late twentieth and early twenty first century concepts of 'emergence'. A cannon ball (using the technology prevalent in Spinoza's time, after it was 'blasted' from the cannon would be in the air for up to a few minutes. If the initial shot cannon ball a few minutes were in a very stretched manner considered as the start of the 'Big Bang' which occurred *vis-a-vis* cannon then in the last million, million, million, millionth of a second let' assume that the cannon-ball (if the Universe, the Earth and humans were to consider conjointly) arose consciousness and were to 'postulate' back to the start of the cannon-shot being fired and the 'conscious stone' would ponder thus: 'the cannon ball could not have fit the mouth of the canon, it could have misfired, it could have dropped on the ground' .It is the concatenation of such impossible odds that I (the cannon ball in the air) can think of my origins and what a wonder that 'I am here!'. This author would emphasise that the Universe postulated age of 13.8 billion years have been encapsulated cannon ball 'traverse' of a few minutes If the initial cannon ball is the 'start' of Universe itself and say the cannon ball flight is 5 min then only in the last 35 to 40 s of the flight has the Earth came into existence and perhaps only in a thousandth or more 1/10,000,000 of a second ago *homosapiens* arose and only perhaps in the last ten millionth or hundredth millionth of a second 1/100,000,000,000,000 of a second or less than that has the 'issue' of emergence or fine-tuning has arisen among a select few humans: a few scientists and philosophers.

Then what would Spinoza have said about the 'emergence' 'fine tuning' contemporary discourse? As stated in an earlier section Spinoza would have to learn about the concept not only of astronomical and geological time and would have to modify, 'fine-tune' (pun intended) or calibrate his concept of *sub specie aeternitatis*. Would he be receptive to emergence concept or the related 'fine tuning' hypothesis? The author repeats that he is aware that Spinoza's example mainly if not exclusively relates to (lack of) human free will v determinism and it is stretched to extrapolate, extend Spinoza's stone example to the contemporary debate and discourses regarding 'emergence'. The writer offers it as a ('sorta') original (if depending on one's perspective and notwithstanding the caveats elaborated above) 'flawed' idea or extension of Spinozism to contemporary 'emergence' notions or stipulations.

The author has ventured to suggest what 'Intelligent designers' would have said to Spinoza's *Deus Sive Natura.* On the obverse side, Spinoza, 'God-intoxicated' person that he was would or could have been skeptical and probably reject the argument of the 'Intelligent designers'. As for Consilience notwithstanding the debates and disagreements among the contemporary philosophers and scientists Spinoza could, in general, favorably look upon 'The Unity of All things' arguably inherent in its concept. Apart from raising the philosophical determinism (as far as – lack of – human free will) is concerned of Spinoza in his 'stone example' and 'stretching' or juxtaposing with the concept of 'emergence' and 'fine-tuning' the author does not venture to 'guess' or take any position on these issues from a Spinozist viewpoint.

8.6 Conclusion

This article apparently a 'spill-over' on-rereading Arnold J. Toynbee's obituary in *Time* have extended to a variety of topics including initially, the brief survey of the philosophies of history including those of Aristotle, Augustine and Marx. A major portion of the first Part of the essay is devoted to the debate between Stephen Jay Gould and Simon Conway Morris on what could be seen as the 'contingent' and 'teleological' views of evolutionary history. The first Part of the Chapter laterally expand these notions to Arnold Toynbee's views of history and also venture to suggest what he might say on this debate.

As to the possible query as to whether the author has made incompatible comparisons he would furnish as a possible justification or additional argument in support of such an exploration from the following observation of Donald Regan. 'the more refined our perception … the less often we are going to find ourselves unable to make comparisons'.[124]

The main protagonists discussed in this essay Arnold J. Toynbee, Stephen Jay Gould, Simon Conway Morris, Ernst Mayr are considered as eminent evolutionary scientists (Mayr, Gould, Conway Morris), historian of human civilizations (Toynbee), historians of science (Mayr, Gould) and philosopher of history (Toynbee), philosopher of biology (Mayr) and political and ethical philosopher (Spinoza). Juxtaposition and extrapolation from excerpts of their writings as well as writings about them have been made with a view to discern or develop a comparative philosophical outlook with excursions into related domains.

The domains of natural history and human history are separate but not entirely delinked disciplines. The juxtaposition of ostensibly disparate but not un-comparable philosophies of history if only putatively and derivatively and despite the obvious

[124]Don Regan, 'Value, Compatibility and Choice', in Ruth Chang (ed), *Incommensurability, Incompatibility and Practical Reason* (Harvard University Press, 1998) 143.

differences between natural and human history has been made. They are made in this chapter (not towards synthesis) or to determine or even discern the 'correct positions'. Instead, regarding the topics discussed, the author has made studied observations and extended comparisons.

Bibliography

Books

Aristotle, *Physics*, tr. CDC Reeve (Hackett Publishing Company, 2018)
Behe, Michael, *Darwin's Black Box: The Biochemical Challenge to Evolution* (Free Press, 1996)
Browne, Lewis, *Spinoza, God-Intoxicated Man: Three Books Which Marks the Three Hundredth Anniversary of the Philosopher's Birth Blessed Spinoza, A Biography* (Macmillan Company, 1932)
Cane, Peter (ed), *The Hart-Fuller Debate in the Twenty-First Century* (Hart Publishing, 2010)
Crick, Francis, *Astonishing Hypothesis: The Scientific Search for the Soul* (Scribner, 1995)
Damasio, Antonio, *Looking for Spinoza: Joy, Sorrow and the Feeling Brain* (Mariner Books, 2003)
Darwin, Charles, *On the Origin of Species by Means of Natural Selection, or the Preservation of Favoured Races in the Struggle for Life* (John Murray, 1sted, 1859)
Davies, Paul, *Cosmic Jackpot: Why Our Universe is Just Right for Life* (Penguin, 2007)
Davies, Paul, *The Accidental Universe* (Cambridge University Press, 1993)
Davis, Percival and Dean H Kenyon, *Of Pandas and People*, Charles Thaxton (ed) (Foundation for Thoughts and Ethics, 1989)
Dawkins, Richard, *The Blind Watchmaker: Why the Evidence of Evolution Reveals a Universe without Design* (Norton and Company, 1986)
Dawkins, Richard, *The God Delusion* (Bantam Books, 2006)
Delcher, Darren, *Consilience for Universal Design: The Emergence of a Third Culture* (Springer Link, 2006)
Dembski, William A, *Intelligent Design: The Bridge between Science and Theology* (Intervarsity Press, 1999)
Dennett, Daniel, *Darwin's Dangerous Idea* (Simon & Schuster, 1995)
Dennett, Daniel, *Consciousness Explained* (Black Bay Book, 1992)
Desai, Meghnad: *Marx's Revenge: The Resurgence of Capitalism and the Death of Statist Socialism* (Verso, 2004).
Eagleton, Terry, *Why Marx Was Right* (Yale University Press, 2011)
Fuller, Lon, *The Morality of Law* (Yale University Press, 1964)
Gould, Stephen Jay, *Rocks of Ages: Science and Religion in the Fullness of Life* (Ballantine Books, 1999)
Gould, Stephen Jay, *Time's Arrow, Time's Cycle: Myth and Metaphor in the Discovery of Geological Time (Jerusalem Harvard Lectures)* (Harvard University Press, 1988)
Gould, Stephen Jay, *Wonderful Life: The Burgess Shale and the Nature of History*, (WW Norton and Company, 1989)
Gullan-Whur, Margaret, *Within Reason: A Life of Spinoza* (St. Martin's Press, 1998)
Hart, HLA, *The Concept of Law* (Oxford Clarendon Law Series, 1951)
Hawking, Stephen, *A Brief History of Time* (Bantam, 1988)
Hawking, Stephen, and Leonard Mlodinow, *The Grand Design* (Bantam, 2010)
Jones, Adam, *Genocide: A Comprehensive Introduction* (Routledge, 2010)
Kuhn, Thomas, *The Structure of Scientific Revolutions* (University of Chicago Press, 1962)

Marx, Karl, *A Contribution to the Critique of Political Economy* (Moscow Progress Publishers, 1977)
Mayr, Ernst, *Systematics and the Origin of Species* (Columbia University Press, 1982)
Mayr, Ernst, *What Evolution Is* (Basic Books, 2001)
Mayr, Ernst, *What Makes Biology Unique: Considerations on the Autonomy of a Scientific Discipline* (Cambridge University Press, 2007)
Morris, Simon Conway, *Life's Solution: Inevitable Humans in a Lonely Universe* (Cambridge University Press, 2004)
Morris, Simon Conway, *The Crucible of Creation: The Burgess Shale and the Rise of Animals* (Oxford University Press, 1998)
Nadler, Steven, *Spinoza: A Life* (Cambridge University Press, 1999)
Nozick, Robert, *Anarchy, State and Utopia* (Basic Books, 1974)
Paley, William, *Natural Theory or Evidence of the Existence and Attributes of the Deity, Collected from the Experiences of Nature* (Oxford University Press, 1802)
Peacock, Roy E, *A Brief History of Eternity, A Considered Response to Stephen Hawking's A Brief History of Time* (Crossway Books, 1990)
Plato, *Crito*, tr Benjamin Jowett (Create Space Independent Publishing, 2015)
Popper, Karl, *Conjectures and Refutations: The Growth of Scientific Knowledge* (Routledge, 2003)
Quigley, John B, *Palestine and Israel, A Challenge to Justice* (Duke University Press, 1990)
Rand, Ayn, *Atlas Shrugged* (Random House, 1957)
Rawls, John, *A Theory of Justice* (Harvard University Press, 1971)
Rees, Martin, *Just Six Numbers the Deep Forces that Shape the Universe* (Basic Books, 2001)
Rocco, Richard J D, *Consilience, Truth and the Mind of God[:] Science, Philosophy and Theology in the Search for Ultimate Meaning* (Springer Link, 2018, corrected publication 2019)
Sheremer, Michael, *The Believing Brain: From Ghosts and Gods to Politics and Conspiracies – How We Construct Belief and Reinforce them as Truths* (Times Publication, 2011)
Spinoza, Benedict de, *The Ethics*, tr RHM Elwes (Wilder Publications, 2007)
St. Augustine, *The City of God Against the Pagans*, tr RW Dyson (Cambridge University Press, 1998)
Stone, Julius, *Israel and Palestine, An Assault on the Law of Nations* (Johns Hopkins University Press, 1982)
Weinberg, Steven, *The First Three Minutes* (Basic Books, 1977)
Whewell, William, *The Philosophy of the Inductive Sciences, Founded Upon Their History* (John W Parker, 1840)
White, James Boyd, *This Book of Starres: Learning to Read George Herbert* (University of Michigan Press, 1995)

Cases

Crosby v National Foreign Trade Council, 530 US 363 (United States Supreme Court)
Edwards v Aguillard, 482 US 578 (United States Supreme Court)
Kitzmiller v. Dover Area School District, 400 F Supp 2d 707 (United States District Court for the Middle District of Pennsylvania)

International Conventions

Convention on the Prevention and Punishment of the Crime of Genocide, 78 United Nations Treaty Series 277

Journal Articles

Alvarez, LW, et al., 'Extraterrestrial Cause for the Cretaceous–Tertiary extinction' (1980) *Science* 208 (4448) 1095–1108
Chown, Marcus, 'Why the Universe Wasn't Fine-Tuned for Life' (2011) 2816 *New Scientist* 5–65
Claeys, P and S Goderis, 'Solar System: Lethal Billiards' (2007) *Nature* 449(7158) 30–31
Fuller, Lon L, 'Positivism and Fidelity to Law - A Reply to Professor Hart' (1958) 71(4) *Harvard Law Review* 630–672
Gould, Stephen Jay, 'Justice Scalia's Misunderstanding' (1987) 87 *Natural History* 137–140
Hart, HLA, 'Positivism and the Separation of Law and Morals' (1958) 71(4) *Harvard Law Review* 593–629
Harvard Law Review Association, 'The Luck of the Law: Allusions to Fortuity in Legal Discourse' (1989) 102(8) *Harvard Law Review* 1862–1882
Lyson, Tyler R, et al., 'Dinosaur Extinction: Closing the "3 m gap"' (13 July 2011) *Biology Letters*, https://doi.org/10.1098/rsbl.2011.0470
Mathews, Peter D, 'Spinoza's Stone: The Logic of Donnie Darko' in (2005) 25(1) *Post Script: Essays in Film and the Humanities* 38
Mayr, Ernst, '80 Years of Watching Evolutionary Scenery' (2004) 305(5680) *Science* 46
Mayr, Ernst, 'Teleological and Teleonomic: A New Analysis' (1974) 14 *Boston Studies in the Philosophy of Science* 91–117
McDonald, J and DJ Mullan, 'Big Bang Nucleo Synthesis: the Strong Nuclear Force Meets the Weak Anthropic Principle' (2009) 80(4) *Physical Review*
Myint Zan, 'Analysis of Aspects of Traditional ("Indigenous") and Western Thinking in the Classical and Modern Burmese Elites Discourse Concerning Madness' (2010) 78 *Akademika (Journal of Southeast Asia Social Sciences and Humanities)*
Self, Janet, '*Bowers vHardwick*: A Study of Aggression' 10(3) *Human Rights Quarterly* 395–432
Shermer, Michael and Frank J Sulloway, 'The Grand Old Man of Evolution' (2000) 8 *Skeptic* 76

Magazine Articles

Beck, Charles, Letters to the Editor, Dover Air Force Base, Del[aware], *Time* (20 June 20 1983)
Clarke, Arthur C, Letters to the Editor, Colombo, Sri Lanka, under the Section 'Iconoclastic Scientist', *Time* (18 July 1983)
Johnson, Philip E, 'Keep the Darwinists Honest', *Citizen* (April 1999)
Sarchet, Penny, 'Why Do We Ignore Warning about Earth's Future' *Slate* (1 February 2015)
Time, 'Education: Vision of God's Creation on the Move' (3 November 1975)
Time, 'Education; Sub Specie Aeternitatis' (7 March 1927)
Time, Books: Prophet of Hope and Fear' (18 October 1954)

Newspaper Articles

Yoon, Carol Kesuk, 'Ernst Mayr, Pioneer in Tracing Geography's Role in the Origin of Species, Dies at 100', *New York Times* (5 February 2005)
Morris, Simon Conway, 'Darwin Was Right. Up to a point', *The Guardian* (12 February 2009)

Websites

Boyle's Lecture, 2005, 'Darwin's Compass; How Evolution Discovers the Song of Creatiob' https://www.giffordlectures.org/lectures/darwins-compass-how-evolution-discovers-song-creation
https://en.wikipedia.org/wiki/Simon_Conway_Morris
Toynbee, Arnold J https://en.wikipedia.org/wiki/Arnold_J._Toynbee

About the Editor

Professor Dr. Myint Zan Professor Dr. Myint Zan has a Bachelor of Arts, Bachelor of Laws from Rangoon University, Burma, Master of Laws from the University of Michigan in the United States, Master of International Law from The Australian National University and Doctor of Philosophy from Griffith University in Australia. From 1989 to 2016 he taught in Law Schools and non-law schools in various Universities in Malaysia, Australia and the South Pacific at undergraduate and graduate levels. His subjects include international law, administrative law, human rights law, international trade and commercial law, legal studies for MBA students, law and society, aspects of South Pacific law, Security and National Defence, Malaysian foreign policy, contract law and jurisprudence. He has published over 90 academic journal articles and chapters in books mainly on aspects of Burmese law and legal history and Asian law, international law, comparative law and human rights law as well as a few on literature and philosophy in journals published in Australia, India, Italy, Malaysia, New Zealand, Singapore, the United Kingdom, the United States and Vanuatu. Since 2017 he has given occasional guest lectures and presentations at the Law, English, Burmese, Philosophy, History and International Relations Departments at the University of Mandalay, University of Toungoo and University of Yangon as well as international conferences in Myanmar and abroad. In 2018 he established the Myint Zan, LLM Prize and Myint Zan LLM fellowship at his alma maters University of Michigan Law School and Myint Zan prize in Law studies at the Faculty of Law, Myint Zan Philosophy Fellowship at the Department of Philosophy at The Australian National University. He has also established two funds: an Honorary Annual Lecture series in the Department of Orthopaedics and a Memorial fund in palliative oncology in memory of his late parents, at their alma mater the University of Pennsylvania School of Medicine. His major academic journal articles are:

M. Zan (ed.), *Legal Education and Legal Traditions: Selected Essays*,
SpringerBriefs in Environment, Security, Development and Peace,
https://doi.org/10.1007/978-3-030-50903-3

- "Some International Law Issues and 'Lessons' from the Cambodian Past", *Malayan Law* (1992) 1, pp. cxiv–clxxi (8 May 1992).
- "US v. Alvarez-Machain 'Kidnap'Case revisited", (1996) 70 (3) *Australian Law Journal* (March 1996) pp. 239–245.
- "Woe Unto Ye Lawyers: Three Royal Orders Concerning Pleaders in early Seventeenth-Century Burma", (2000) 44 (1) *The American Journal of Legal History*, pp 40–72.
- "The Three Nixon Cases and their Parallels in Malaysia", (2001) 13 (2) *St. Thomas Law Review*, pp 743–784.
- Interview by Eric Yoon Joong Lee and Stewart Manley 'International Lawyer: A Dialogue with Judicial Wisdom: Professor Dr. Myint Zan', (2018) 11 (2) *Journal of East Asia and International Law*, pp. 499–512.

Address: Professor Dr. Myint Zan, c/o Dr Aye Aye Win, 33 E Bogyoke Aung San Museum Street, Bo Choe Quarters, Bahan Township, Yangon 11021, Myanmar

Email: myintzan@yahoo.com.au

Websites: https://law.anu.edu.au/alumni/alumni-profiles/professor-myint-zan; https://www.researchgate.net/profile/Myint_Zan and https://mmu-my.academia.edu/MyintZan.

About the Authors

Charlene Constance Chai graduated with a LL.B from Multimedia University in Malacca, Malaysia and has practiced law with the law firm of Kuek, Ong and Associates in Petaling Jaya, Malaysia.

Email: Charlene.chai.91@gmail.com

Chew Yi Ting graduated from Multimedia University (MMU) in Malacca with a LL.B. Currently she practices as an advocate and solicitor in the High Court of Malaya under her own legal firm, Yiting Law Office. She was awarded a Diploma in International Arbitration accredited by Chartered Institute of Arbitrators (CIArb).

Email: yiting1992@gmail.com

Chong Jun Min is currently a practicing advocate and solicitor at Messr JA Yeoh, Penang, Malaysia. She was called to the Malaysian Bar in 2018. She has a LL.B from University of London in 2012 and another LL.B from Multimedia University in 2017.

Email: junmin@jayeoh.com

Dr. Mary George is a Professor in the Faculty of Law, University of Malaya, Kuala Lumpur, Malaysia. She has a B.Sc. from Kerala University, LL.B from Bangalore University, LL.M from the London School of Political Science and a Ph.D. from the University of Sydney, Australia. She has published books and journal articles in Criminal Law, Equity and Trusts. Law of the Sea and International Law.

Email: maryg@um.edu.my

Kan Da Xing graduated with a LLB from Multimedia University in 2015. He was admitted as an Advocate and Solicitor in the High Court of Malaya in 2016. Currently

M. Zan (ed.), *Legal Education and Legal Traditions: Selected Essays*,
SpringerBriefs in Environment, Security, Development and Peace,
https://doi.org/10.1007/978-3-030-50903-3

he practices in the law firm of Ven Nie & Kan Associates in Kuala Lumpur as an Advocate and Solicitor.

Email: vennie.co@gmail.com

Dr. Dennis Wye Keen Khong is an Associate Professor at the Faculty of Law, Multimedia University, Malacca, Malaysia. He has a LL.B from the University of Malaya, a European Master in Law and Economics from the University of Hamburg, and Doctor of Philosophy from the University of Strathclyde. His research interests are law and economics, intellectual property law, technology law, and legal technology, including application of machine learning to legal research.

Email: wkkhong@mmu.edu.my

Stewart Manley is a Lecturer at the Faculty of Law, University of Malaya, Kuala Lumpur, Malaysia. He also taught at the Faculty of Law, Multimedia University, Malacca, Malaysia, worked for the Burma Lawyers' Council in Mae Sot, Thailand, and practiced law at Jennings, Strouss and Salmon in Phoenix, Arizona, USA. His research focuses on international criminal law, trust law, and the laws and ethics of scholarly publishing.

Email: stewart.manley@um.edu.my

Dr. Gita Radhakrishna graduated with LLB (London, Honours) in 1981, completed her Bar at the Middle Temple and was called to the High Court of Malaya in 1983. She practiced law for several years. She currently lectures at the Faculty of Law at Multimedia University where she completed her MPhil. and her Ph.D. Her areas of research includes electronic evidence and e-discovery, Insolvency Law, Conveyancing Practice, Banking Law, Professional Practice, and Privacy.

Email: gita.radhakrishna@mmu.edu.my

About the Book

This book deals with aspects of legal education and legal traditions. Part I includes chapters on teaching Law of the Sea, legal ethics and educating lawyers as 'transaction cost engineers' as well as comparison of teaching law in a refugee camp and in a Malaysian University. Part II on legal and philosophical traditions includes essays on what later philosophers would have commented on Plato's arguments in the *Crito* regarding 'absolute obligation to obey the law' and what Socrates would have said on two conversations in the 19th century novel *Uncle Tom's Cabin* regarding the morality and legality of harbouring runaway slaves. Part II concludes with two essays regarding the applicability of the Hart-Devlin debate on the 'enforcement of morals' vis-à-vis the International Criminal Court and an essay on what the historian Arnold Toynbee would have commented on the 'contingency' v 'teleology' debate between two palaeontologists the late Stephen Jay Gould and Simon Conway Morris.

- Legal education of interest to legal educators and students
- Legal, political, moral philosophy as well as philosophy of history of interest to law, philosophy and history teachers, postgraduate and under graduate students
- Aspects of legal ethics for law teachers, students and legal professionals
- Interdisciplinary studies regarding law and economics, law and literature, law and social justice for law, humanities, social science academics and students.

M. Zan (ed.), *Legal Education and Legal Traditions: Selected Essays*,
SpringerBriefs in Environment, Security, Development and Peace,
https://doi.org/10.1007/978-3-030-50903-3

The manufacturer's authorised representative in the EU is Springer Nature Customer Service Centre GmbH, Europaplatz 3, 69115 Heidelberg, Germany. If you have any concerns regarding our products, please contact ProductSafety@springernature.com

Printed and bound by CPI Group (UK) Ltd, Croydon, CR0 4YY
30/09/2026
02225467-0011